Best Stories of Saki

Abridged Version

V&S PUBLISHERS

Published by:

V&S PUBLISHERS

F-2/16, Ansari road, Daryaganj, New Delhi-110002
☎ 23240026, 23240027 • *Fax:* 011-23240028
Email: info@vspublishers.com • *Website:* www.vspublishers.com

Regional Office : Hyderabad
5-1-707/1, Brij Bhawan (Beside Central Bank of India Lane)
Bank Street, Koti, Hyderabad - 500 095
☎ 040-24737290
E-mail: vspublishershyd@gmail.com

Branch Office : Mumbai
Jaywant Industrial Estate, 2nd Floor-222, Tardeo Road
Opposite Sobo Central, Mumbai - 400 034
☎ 022-23510736
E-mail: vspublishersmum@gmail.com

Follow us on: 🅃 🅵 🅸🅽

All books available at **www.vspublishers.com**

Printed at : Repro Knowledgecast Limited, Thane

Publisher's Note

It has been our constant endeavour at the **V&S Publishers** to publish all kinds of books ranging from Fiction, Non-fiction, Storybooks, Children Encyclopaedias, to Self-Help, Science Books, Dictionaries, Grammar Books, Self-Development, Management Books, etc.

However, this is for the first time that we are venturing into the vast, rich ocean of English Literature and have come up with this book authored by saki. There is a lot to learn from their writing style, selection of plot, development and building of theme and suspense of the story, emphasis and presentation of characters, dialogues, working towards the climax of the story, presenting the climax, and then finally concluding the story.

Besides the above mentioned characteristics, the book contains a short biography of the author, his brief life history, notable works and literary achievements. Each story has a set of word meanings on each page.

These books are not only a boon for the school-going students, particularly studying in senior classes from the seventh standard till the twelfth, but are also a treasure trove for all those young and aspiring writers, voracious readers and lovers of English language and literature.

Contents

Saki

Born on December 18, 1870
Died on November 13, 1916
Pen name: Saki
Notable Works: *The Rise of the Russian Empire, The Woman Who Never Should, The Not So Stories, Reginald in Russia The Chronicles of Clovis* (short stories), *The Unbearable Bassington, When William Came, Beasts and Super-Beasts, The East Wing, The Interlopers, The Watched Pot, The Toys of Peace, The Storyteller, The Open Window, Esme, The East Wing and many more.*

Early Life

Hector Hugh Munro, better known by the pen name, *Saki*, and also frequently as *H. H. Munro*, was a British writer, whose witty, mischievous and sometimes macabre stories satirised Edwardian society and culture. He is considered a master of the short story and often compared to O. Henry and Dorothy Parker. Influenced by Oscar Wilde, Lewis Carroll, and Kipling, he himself influenced A. A. Milne, Noël Coward, and P. G. Wodehouse.

Born in Akyab, Burma (now known as Myanmar), when it was still part of the British Empire, Hector Hugh Munro was the son of Charles Augustus Munro and Mary Frances Mercer.

Munro was educated at Pencarwick School in Exmouth, Devon and at Bedford School. On a few occasions, when he retired, Charles travelled with Hector and his sister to fashionable European spas and tourist resorts. In 1893, Hector followed his father into the Indian Imperial Police, where he was posted to Burma. Two years later, having contracted malaria, he resigned and returned to England.

At the start of World War I, although 43 and officially overage, Munro refused a commission and joined the British Army Royal Fusiliers as an ordinary soldier. More than once, he returned to the battlefield when officially still too sick or injured.

Literary Works and Achievements

In England, he started his career as a journalist, writing for newspapers, such as the *Westminster Gazette*, *Daily Express*, *Bystander*, *Morning Post* and *Outlook*. In 1900, Munro's first book appeared: *The Rise of the Russian Empire.* Shortly before the Great War, with the genre of invasion literature selling well, he also published a W*hat-if* novel. Beside his short stories (which were first published in newspapers, as was customary at the time, and then collected into several volumes), he wrote a full-length play, *The Watched Pot*, in collaboration with Charles Maude; two one-act plays; a historical study, *The Rise of the Russian Empire,* the only book published under his own name; a short novel, *The Unbearable Bassington; A Story of London Under the Hohenzollerns*, which was a fantasy about a future German invasion of Britain, etc. Among his popular short stories are: *The Interlopers, Gabriel-Ernest, The Toys of Peace, The Storyteller, The Open Window, The Unrest-Cure, Esme, The East Wing and many more.*

Later Years

In November 1916, Saki was sheltering in a shell crater near Beaumont-Hamel, France, when he was killed by a German sniper. After his death, his sister Ethel destroyed most of his papers and wrote her own account of their childhood.

Trivia

To recognise his contribution to English literature, **a blue plaque** has been affixed to a building in which Munro once lived on Mortimer Street in central London.

Canossa

~ Saki

DEmosthenes Platterbaff, the eminent Unrest Inducer, stood on his trial for a serious offence, and the eyes of the political world were focussed on the jury. The offence, it should be stated, was serious for the Government rather than for the prisoner. He had blown up the Albert Hall on the eve of the great Liberal Federation Tango Tea, the occasion on which the Chancellor of the Exchequer was expected to propound his new theory: "Do *partridges* spread infectious diseases?" Platterbaff had chosen his time well; the Tango Tea had been hurriedly postponed, but there were other political fixtures which could not be put off under any circumstances. The day after the trial there was to be a by-election at Nemesis-on-Hand, and it had been openly announced in the division that if Platterbaff were languishing in gaol on polling day the Government candidate would be "outed" to a certainty. Unfortunately, there could be no doubt or *misconception* as to Platterbaff's guilt.

He had not only pleaded guilty, but had expressed his intention of repeating his escapade in other directions as soon as circumstances permitted; throughout the trial he was busy examining a small model of the Free Trade Hall in Manchester. The jury could not possibly find that the prisoner had not deliberately and intentionally blown up the Albert Hall; the question was: Could they find any extenuating circumstances which would permit of an acquittal? Of course any sentence which the law might feel compelled to inflict would be followed by an immediate pardon, but it was highly desirable, from the Government's point of view, that the necessity for such an exercise of clemency should not arise. A *headlong* pardon, on the eve of a by-election, with threats of a heavy voting defection if it were withheld or even delayed, would not necessarily be a surrender, but it would look like one. *Opponents* would be only too ready to attribute ungenerous motives. Hence the anxiety in the crowded Court, and in the little groups gathered round the tape-machines in Whitehall and Downing Street and other affected centres.

The jury returned from considering their verdict; there was a flutter, an excited murmur, a death-like *hush*. The foreman delivered his message:

"The jury find the prisoner guilty of blowing up the Albert Hall. The jury wish to add a rider drawing attention to the fact

Partridges - *Small old world game birds*
Headlong - *Without delay, hastily, plunge*
Misconception - *False notion*
Opponents - *Competitions*

that a by-election is pending in the Parliamentary division of Nemesis-on-Hand."

"That, of course," said the Government Prosecutor, springing to his feet, "is equivalent to an *acquittal?*"

"I hardly think so," said the Judge, coldly; "I feel obliged to sentence the prisoner to a week's imprisonment."

"And may the Lord have mercy on the poll," a Junior Counsel exclaimed irreverently. It was a scandalous sentence, but then the Judge was not on the Ministerial side in politics. The verdict and sentence were made known to the public at twenty minutes past five in the afternoon; at half-past five a dense crowd was *massed* outside the Prime Minister's residence lustily singing, to the air of "Trelawney":

> "And should our Hero rot in gaol,
>
> For e'en a single day,
>
> There's Fifteen Hundred Voting Men
>
> Will vote the other way."

"Fifteen hundred," said the Prime Minister, with a shudder; "it's too horrible to think of. Our majority last time was only a thousand and seven."

"The poll opens at eight to-morrow morning," said the Chief Organiser; "we must have him out by 7 a.m."

"Seven-thirty," amended the Prime Minister; "we must avoid any appearance of precipitancy."

"Not later than seven-thirty, then," said the Chief Organiser; "I have promised the agent down there that he shall be able to display posters announcing 'Platterbaff is Out,' before the poll opens. He said it was our only chance of getting a telegram 'Radprop is In' to-night."

At half-past seven the next morning the Prime Minister and the Chief Organiser sat at breakfast, making a perfunctory meal, and awaiting the return of the Home Secretary, who had gone in person to superintend, the releasing of Platterbaff. Despite the earliness of the hour a small crowd had gathered in the street outside, and the horrible *menacing* Trelawney *refrain* of the "Fifteen Hundred Voting Men" came in a steady, *monotonous* chant.

"They will cheer presently when they hear the news," said the Prime Minister hopefully; "hark! They are *booing* some one now! That must be McKenna."

The Home Secretary entered the room a moment later, disaster written on his face.

"He won't go!" he exclaimed.

Acquittal - *The deliverance/release a person before a court*

Massed - *Heap/Pile*

Menacing - *Extremely annoying person*

Refrainent - *Desist, Forbear*

Monotonous - *Boring, dull*

"Won't go? Won't leave gaol?"

"He won't go unless he has a brass band. He says he never has left prison without a brass band to play him out, and he's not going to go without one now."

"But surely that sort of thing is provided by his supporters and admirers?" said the Prime Minister; "we can hardly be supposed to supply a released prisoner with a brass band. How on earth could we defend it on the Estimates?"

"His supporters say it is up to us to provide the music," said the Home Secretary; "they say we put him in prison, and it's our affair to see that he leaves it in a respectable manner. Anyway, he won't go unless he has a band."

The telephone *squealed shrilly*; it was a trunk call from Nemesis.

"Poll opens in five minutes. Is Platterbaff out yet? In Heaven's name, why --"

The Chief Organiser rang off.

"This is not a moment for standing on dignity," he observed *bluntly*; "musicians must be supplied at once. Platterbaff must have his band."

"Where are you going to find the musicians?" asked the Home Secretary *wearily*; "we can't employ a military band, in fact, I don't think he'd have one if we offered it, and there ain't any others. There's a musicians' strike on, I suppose you know."

"Can't you get a strike permit?" asked the Organiser.

"I'll try," said the Home Secretary, and went to the telephone.

Eight o'clock struck. The crowd outside chanted with an increasing volume of sound:

"Will vote the other way."

A telegram was brought in. It was from the central committee rooms at Nemesis. "Losing twenty votes per minute," was its brief message.

Ten o'clock struck. The Prime Minister, the Home Secretary, the Chief Organiser, and several earnest helpful friends were gathered in the inner gateway of the prison, talking volubly to Demosthenes Platterbaff, who stood with folded arms and squarely planted feet, silent in their midst. Golden-tongued legislators whose *eloquence* had *swayed* the Marconi Inquiry Committee, or at any rate the greater part of it, expended their arts of oratory in vain on this stubborn unyielding man. Without a band he would not go; and they had no band.

Booing - *To shout and express disgust*
Bluntly - *Rudely*
Squaled - *Sudden violent gust of wind*
Shrilly - *High pitched voice*
Wearily - *Tiredly*

A quarter past ten, half-past. A constant stream of tele-graph boys poured in through the prison gates.

"Yamley's factory hands just voted you can guess how," ran a despairing message, and the others were all of the same *tenour*. Nemesis was going the way of Reading.

"Have you any band instruments of an easy nature to play?" demanded the Chief Organiser of the Prison Governor; "drums, *cymbals*, those sort of things?"

"The warders have a private band of their own," said the Governor, "but of course I couldn't allow the men themselves --"

"Lend us the instruments," said the Chief Organiser.

One of the earnest helpful friends was a skilled performer on the cornet, the Cabinet Ministers were able to clash cymbals more or less in tune, and the Chief Organiser has some knowl-edge of the drum.

"What tune would you prefer?" he asked Platterbaff.

"The popular song of the moment," replied the Agitator after a moment's reflection. It was a tune they had all heard hundreds of times, so there was no difficulty in turning out a *passable* imitation of it. To the improvised strains of "I didn't want to do it" the prisoner strode forth to freedom. The word of the song had reference, it was understood, to the incarcer-ating Government and not to the destroyer of the Albert Hall.

The seat was lost, after all, by a narrow majority. The local Trade Unionists took offence at the fact of Cabinet Ministers having personally acted as strike-breakers, and even the re-lease of Platterbaff failed to pacify them. The seat was lost, but Ministers had scored a moral victory. They had shown that they knew when and how to *yield.*

Food For Thought

Why do you think the Prime Minister released Platterbaff from jail and also asked the Brass Band to play him out? The Cabinet Ministers and the Prime Minister lost the elections but won the people's hearts. Do you agree? Support your answer with relevant reasons.

Eloquence - *Ease in using language to the best effect*
Swayed - *To move or swing to one side or in one direction*
Tenor - *Period*
Cymbals - *Percussion instruments of indefinite pitch*
Passable - *Adequate, acceptable*

Bertie's Christmas Eve

~ Saki

IT was Christmas Eve, and the family circle of Luke Stef-fink, Esq., was aglow with the amiability and random *mirth* which the occasion demanded. A long and lavish dinner had been *partaken* of, waits had been round and sung carols; the house-party had regaled itself with more *caroling* on its own account, and there had been romping which, even in a pulpit reference, could not have been condemned as *ragging*. In the midst of the general glow, however, there was one black unkindled cinder.

Bertie Steffink, nephew of the *aforementioned* Luke, had early in life adopted the profession of ne'er-do-weel; his father had been something of the kind before him. At the age of eighteen Bertie had commenced that round of visits to our Colonial possessions, so seemly and desirable in the case of a Prince of the Blood, so suggestive of insincerity in a young man of the middle-class. He had gone to grow tea in Ceylon and fruit in British Columbia, and to help sheep to grow wool in Australia. At the age of twenty he had just returned from some similar errand in Canada, from which it may be gathered that the trial he gave to these various experiments was of the summary drum-head nature. Luke Steffink, who fulfilled the troubled role of guardian and deputy-parent to Bertie, deplored the persistent manifestation of the homing instinct on his nephew's part, and his solemn thanks earlier in the day for the blessing of reporting a united family had no reference to Bertie's return.

Arrangements had been promptly made for packing the youth off to a distant corner of Rhodesia, whence return would be a difficult matter; the journey to this uninviting destination was imminent, in fact a more careful and willing traveller would have already begun to think about his packing. Hence Bertie was in no mood to share in the festive spirit which displayed itself around him, and *resentment smouldered* within him at the eager, self-absorbed discussion of social plans for the coming months which he heard on all sides. Beyond depressing his uncle and the family circle generally by singing "Say au revoir, and not good-bye," he had taken no part in the evening's *conviviality*.

Aforementioned
- *Mentioned before*
Resentment - *M*
Caroling - *Singing a christmas song/hymn*
Ragging - *Teasing*

Eleven o'clock had struck some half-hour ago, and the elder Steffinks began to throw out suggestions leading up to that process which they called retiring for the night.

"Come, Teddie, it's time you were in your little bed, you know," said Luke Steffink to his thirteen-year-old son.

"That's where we all ought to be," said Mrs. Steffink.

"There wouldn't be room," said Bertie.

The remark was considered to border on the scandalous; everybody ate **raisins** and almonds with the nervous industry of sheep feeding during threatening weather.

"In Russia," said Horace Bordenby, who was staying in the house as a Christmas guest, "I've read that the peasants believe that if you go into a cow-house or stable at midnight on Christmas Eve you will hear the animals talk. They're supposed to have the gift of speech at that one moment of the year."

"Oh, DO let's ALL go down to the cow-house and listen to what they've got to say!" exclaimed Beryl, to whom anything was thrilling and amusing if you did it in a troop.

Mrs. Steffink made a laughing protest, but gave a virtual consent by saying, "We must all wrap up well, then." The idea seemed a **scatterbrained** one to her, and almost heathenish, but if afforded an opportunity for "throwing the young people together," and as such she welcomed it. Mr. Horace Bordenby was a young man with quite **substantial** prospects, and he had danced with Beryl at a local **subscription** ball a sufficient number of times to warrant the authorised inquiry on the part of the neighbours whether "there was anything in it." Though Mrs. Steffink would not have put it in so many words, she shared the idea of the Russian peasantry that on this night the beast might speak.

The cow-house stood at the junction of the garden with a small **paddock**, an isolated survival, in a suburban neighbourhood; of what had once been a small farm. Luke Steffink was **complacently** proud of his cow-house and his two cows; he felt that they gave him a stamp of solidity which no number of Wyandottes or Orpingtons could impart. They even seemed to link him in a sort of **inconsequent** way with those **patriarchs** who derived importance from their floating capital of flocks and herds, he-asses and she-asses. It had been an anxious and **momentous** occasion when he had had to decide definitely

Raisins - *Dried grapes*
Substantial - *Enough*
Paddock - *A small usually enclosed field near a stable/barn*
Complacently - *Pleasantly*

between "the Byre" and "the Ranch" for the naming of his villa residence. A December midnight was hardly the moment he would have chosen for showing his farm-building to visitors, but since it was a fine night, and the young people were anxious for an excuse for a mild *frolic*, Luke consented to chaperon the *expedition*. The servants had long since gone to bed, so the house was left in charge of Bertie, who *scornfully* declined to stir out on the pretext of listening to *bovine* conversation.

"We must go quietly," said Luke, as he headed the *procession* of *giggling* young folk, brought up in the rear by the shawled and *hooded* figure of Mrs. Steffink; "I've always laid stress on keeping this a quiet and orderly neighbourhood."

It was a few minutes to midnight when the party reached the cow-house and made its way in by the light of Luke's stable lantern. For a moment every one stood in silence, almost with a feeling of being in church.

"Daisy -- the one lying down -- is by a shorthorn bull out of a Guernsey cow," announced Luke in a hushed voice, which was in keeping with the *foregoing* impression.

"Is she?" said Bordenby, rather as if he had expected her to be by Rembrandt.

"Myrtle is --"

Myrtle's family history was cut short by a little scream from the women of the party.

The cow-house door had closed noiselessly behind them and the key had turned *gratingly* in the lock; then they heard Bertie's voice pleasantly wishing them good-night and his footsteps retreating along the garden path.

Luke Steffink strode to the window; it was a small square opening of the old-fashioned sort, with iron bars let into the stonework.

"Unlock the door this instant," he shouted, with as much air of menacing authority as a hen might assume when screaming through the bars of a coop at a *marauding* hawk. In reply to his summons the hall-door closed with a *defiant* bang.

A neighbouring clock struck the hour of midnight. If the cows had received the gift of human speech at that moment they would not have been able to make themselves heard. Seven or eight other voices were engaged in describing Bertie's present conduct and his general character at a high pressure of excitement and *indignation*.

Frolic - *Merriment, fun, prank*
Expedition - *An excursion*
Scornfuly - *Contemptuously*
Bovine - *Stolid, dull*
Cession - *Surrender*

In the course of half an hour or so everything that it was permissible to say about Bertie had been said some dozens of times, and other topics began to come to the front -- the extreme *mustiness* of the cow-house, the possibility of it catching fire, and the probability of it being a Rowton House for the vagrant rats of the neighbourhood. And still no sign of deliverance came to the unwilling *vigil-keepers.*

Towards one o'clock the sound of rather boisterous and undisciplined carol-singing approached rapidly, and came to a sudden *anchorage*, apparently just outside the garden-gate. A motor-load of youthful "bloods," in a high state of conviviality, had made a temporary halt for repairs; the stoppage, however, did not extend to the vocal efforts of the party, and the watchers in the cow-shed were treated to a highly unauthorised rendering of "Good King Wenceslas," in which the adjective "good" appeared to be very carelessly applied.

The noise had the effect of bringing Bertie out into the garden, but he utterly ignored the pale, angry faces peering out at the cow-house window, and concentrated his attention on the *revellers* outside the gate.

"Wassail, you chaps!" he shouted.

"Wassail, old sport!" they shouted back; "we'd jolly well drink y'r health, only we've nothing to drink it in."

"Come and *wassail* inside," said Bertie *hospitably*; "I'm all alone, and there's heap's of 'wet'."

They were total strangers, but his touch of kindness made them instantly his kin. In another moment the unauthorised version of King Wenceslas, which, like many other scandals, grew worse on repetition, went echoing up the garden path; two of the revellers gave an *impromptu* performance on the way by executing the staircase waltz up the terraces of what Luke Steffink, hitherto with some justification, called his rock-garden. The rock part of it was still there when the waltz had been accorded its third encore. Luke, more than ever like a cooped hen behind the cow-house bars, was in a position to realise the feelings of concert-goers unable to *countermand* the call for an encore which they neither desire or deserve.

The hall door closed with a bang on Bertie's guests, and the sounds of merriment became faint and *muffled* to the weary watchers at the other end of the garden. Presently two *ominous* pops, in quick succession, made themselves distinctly heard.

Mustiness - *Out of date*
Anchorage - *A charge for occupying such an area*
Wassail - *An alcholic drink*
Ominous - *Foreboding evil*
Impromptu - *Made/done without preparation*

"They've got at the champagne!" exclaimed Mrs. Steffink.

"Perhaps it's the sparkling Moselle," said Luke hopefully. Three or four more pops were heard.

"The *champagne* and the sparkling *Moselle*," said Mrs. Steffink.

Luke uncorked an expletive which, like brandy in a temperance household, was only used on rare emergencies. Mr. Horace Bordenby had been making use of similar expressions under his breath for a considerable time past. The experiment of "throwing the young people together" had been prolonged beyond a point when it was likely to produce any romantic result.

Some forty minutes later the hall door opened and disgorged a crowd that had thrown off any restraint of shyness that might have influenced its earlier actions. Its vocal efforts in the direction of carol singing were now *supplemented* by instrumental music; a Christmas-tree that had been prepared for the children of the gardener and other household retainers had yielded a rich spoil of tin trumpets, rattles, and drums. The life-story of King Wenceslas had been dropped, Luke was thankful to notice, but it was intensely irritating for the chilled prisoners in the cow-house to be told that it was a hot time in the old town tonight, together with some accurate but entirely superfluous information as to the imminence of Christmas morning. Judging by the protests which began to be shouted from the upper windows of neighbouring houses the sentiments prevailing in the cow-house were heartily echoed in other quarters.

The revellers found their car, and, what was more remarkable, managed to drive off in it, with a parting fanfare of tin trumpets. The lively beat of a drum disclosed the fact that the master of the revels remained on the scene.

"Bertie!" came in an angry, *imploring* chorus of shouts and screams from the cow-house window.

"Hullo," cried the owner of the name, turning his rather *errant* steps in the direction of the summons; "are you people still there? Must have heard everything cows got to say by this time. If you haven't, no use waiting. After all, it's a Russian legend, and *Russian Chrismush Eve* not due for 'nother fortnight. Better come out."

Champagne - *The speaking dry, white table*

Moselle - *A light, white wine of Germany*

Supplemented - *Added*

Imploring - *To beg earnestly*

Errant - *Moving aimlessly*

Ineffectual -
Inefficient, inept
Lusty - *Greedy*
Accompaniment
- *Complement,*
supplement
Exuberant - *Full of*
enregy, cheerful
Rotten - *Decayed*

After one or two ineffectual attempts he managed to pitch the key of the cow-house door in through the window. Then, lifting his voice in the strains of "I'm afraid to go home in the dark," with a lusty drum accompaniment, he led the way back to the house. The hurried procession of the released that followed in his steps came in for a good deal of the adverse comment that his exuberant display had evoked.

It was the happiest Christmas Eve he had ever spent. To quote his own words, he had a rotten Christmas.

Food For Thought

How did Bertie enjoy his Christmas eve? How did the revellers join him and what did Bertie and the revellers do while the elders were away in the cow-house waiting anxiously for the animals to talk after midnight? Do you believe that such things do happen even in this modern age?

Esme

~ Saki

"All hunting stories are the same," said Clovis; "just as all Turf stories are the same, and all--"

"My hunting story isn't a bit like any you've ever heard," said the Baroness. "It happened quite a while ago, when I was about twenty-three. I wasn't living apart from my husband then; you see, neither of us could afford to make the other a separate allowance. In spite of everything that proverbs may say, poverty keeps together more homes than it breaks up. But we always hunted with different packs. All this has nothing to do with the story."

"We haven't arrived at the meet yet. I suppose there was a meet," said Clovis.

"Of course there was a meet," said the Baroness; "all the usual crowd were there, especially Constance Broddle. Constance is one of those *strapping* florid girls that go so well with autumn scenery or Christmas decorations in church. 'I feel a *presentiment* that something dreadful is going to happen,' she said to me; 'am I looking pale?'

"She was looking about as pale as a beetroot that has suddenly heard bad news.

" 'You're looking nicer than usual,' I said, 'but that's so easy for you.' Before she had got the right bearings of this remark we had settled down to business; hounds had found a fox lying out in some gorse-bushes."

"I knew it," said Clovis; "in every fox-hunting story that I've ever heard there's been a fox and some gorse-bushes."

"Constance and I were well mounted," continued the Baroness serenely, "and we had no difficulty in keeping ourselves in the first flight, though it was a fairly stiff run. Towards the finish, however, we must have held rather too independent a line, for we lost the hounds, and found ourselves *plodding* aimlessly along miles away from anywhere. It was fairly *exasperating*, and my temper was beginning to let itself go by

Strapping - *Powerfully*
Presentiment - *Foreboding*
Plodding - *To walk heavily*
Exasperating - *To irritate, provoke built*

inches, when on pushing our way through an accommodating hedge we were gladdened by the sight of hounds in full cry in a hollow just beneath us.

" 'There they go,' cried Constance, and then added in a gasp, 'In Heaven's name, what are they hunting?'

"It was certainly no mortal fox. It stood more than twice as high, had a short, ugly head, and an enormous thick neck.

" 'It's a hyena,' I cried; 'it must have escaped from Lord Pabham's Park.'

"At that moment the hunted beast turned and faced its *pursuers*, and the *hounds* (there were only about six couple of them) stood round in a half-circle and looked foolish. Evidently, they had broken away from the rest of the pack on the trail of this alien scent, and were not quite sure how to treat their *quarry* now they had got him.

"The hyena hailed our approach with unmistakable relief and demonstrations of friendliness. It had probably been accustomed to uniform kindness from humans, while its first experience of a pack of hounds had left a bad impression. The hounds looked more than ever embarrassed as their quarry paraded its sudden intimacy with us, and the faint toot of a horn in the distance was seized on as a welcome signal for *unobtrusive* departure. Constance and I and the hyena were left alone in the gathering twilight.

" 'What are we to do?' asked Constance.

" 'What a person you are for questions,' I said.

" 'Well, we can't stay here all night with a hyena,' she retorted.

" 'I don't know what your ideas of comfort are,' I said; 'but I shouldn't think of staying here all night even without a hyena. My home may be an unhappy one, but at least it has hot and cold water laid on, and domestic service, and other conveniences which we shouldn't find here. We had better make for that ridge of trees to the right; I imagine the Crowley road is just beyond.'

"We *trotted* off slowly along a faintly marked cart-track, with the beast following cheerfully at our heels.

" 'What on earth are we to do with the hyena?' came the *inevitable* question.

Strapping -
Powerfully
Presentiment -
Foreboding
Plodding - *To walk heavily*
Exasperating - *To irritate, provoke built*

" 'What does one generally do with hyenas?' I asked crossly.

" 'I've never had anything to do with one before,' said Constance.

" 'Well, neither have I. If we even knew its sex we might give it a name. Perhaps we might call it Esme. That would do in either case.

"There was still sufficient daylight for us to distinguish wayside objects, and our listless spirits gave an upward perk as we came upon a small half-naked gipsy brat picking blackberries from a low-growing bush.

The sudden *apparition* of two horsewomen and a hyena set it off crying, and in any case we should scarcely have gleaned any useful geographical information from that source; but there was a probability that we might strike a gipsy *encampment* somewhere along our route. We rode on hopefully but uneventfully for another mile or so.

" 'I wonder what the child was doing there,' said Constance presently.

" 'Picking blackberries. Obviously.'

" 'I don't like the way it cried,' pursued Constance; 'somehow its wail keeps ringing in my ears.'

"I did not chide Constance for her morbid fancies; as a matter of fact the same sensation, of being pursued by a *persistent fretful wail*, had been forcing itself on my rather over-tired nerves. For company's sake I hulloed to Esme, who had lagged somewhat behind. With a few springy bounds he drew up level, and then shot past us.

"The wailing accompaniment was explained. The gipsy child was firmly, and I expect painfully, held in his jaws.

" 'Merciful Heaven!' screamed Constance, 'what on earth shall we do? What are we to do?'

"I am perfectly certain that at the Last Judgment Constance will ask more questions than any of the examining Seraphs.

" 'Can't we do something?' she persisted tearfully, as Esme cantered easily along in front of our tired horses.

"Personally I was doing everything that occurred to me at the moment. I stormed and scolded and *coaxed* in English and

Apparition - *A supernatural appearance of a person*
Encampment - *The act of setting up a camp*
Persistent - *Lasting*
Coaxed - *To influence*
Lumbered - *To put timber*

French and gamekeeper language; I made absurd, ineffectual cuts in the air with my thongless hunting-crop; I hurled my sandwich case at the brute; in fact, I really don't know what more I could have done. And still we *lumbered* on through the deepening dusk, with that dark uncouth shape lumbering ahead of us, and a drone of lugubrious music floating in our ears.

Suddenly Esme bounded aside into some thick bushes, where we could not follow; the wail rose to a *shriek* and then stopped altogether. This part of the story I always hurry over, because it is really rather horrible. When the beast joined us again, after an absence of a few minutes, there was an air of patient understanding about him, as though he knew that he had done something of which we disapproved, but which he felt to be thoroughly justifiable.

" 'How can you let that *ravening* beast trot by your side?' asked Constance. She was looking more than ever like an albino beetroot.

" 'In the first place, I can't prevent it,' I said; 'and in the second place, whatever else he may be, I doubt if he's ravening at the present moment.'

"Constance *shuddered*. 'Do you think the poor little thing suffered much?' came another of her futile questions.

" 'The indications were all that way,' I said; 'on the other hand, of course, it may have been crying from sheer temper. Children sometimes do.'

"It was nearly pitch-dark when we emerged suddenly into the high road. A flash of lights and the whir of a motor went past us at the same moment at uncomfortably close quarters. A thud and a sharp screeching yell followed a second later. The car drew up, and when I had ridden back to the spot I found a young man bending over a dark motionless mass lying by the roadside.

" 'You have killed my Esme,' I exclaimed bitterly.

" 'I'm so awfully sorry,' said the young man; 'I keep dogs myself, so I know what you must feel about it. I'll do anything I can in reparation.'

Shriek - *Loud noised*
Ravening - *Voracious*
Interments - *Firmly resolved*
Contingencies - *Facts/ events*
Resolutely - *The act/ ceremony of burial*

" 'Please bury him at once,' I said; 'that much I think I may ask of you.

" 'Bring the spade, William,' he called to the chauffeur. Evidently hasty roadside *interments* were *contingencies* that had been provided against.

"The digging of a sufficiently large grave took some little time. 'I say, what a magnificent fellow,' said the motorist as the corpse was rolled over into the trench. 'I'm afraid he must have been rather a valuable animal.'

" 'He took second in the puppy class at Birmingham last year,' I said *resolutely*.

Constance *snorted* loudly.

"'Don't cry, dear,' I said brokenly; 'it was all over in a moment. He couldn't have suffered much.'

"'Look here,' said the young fellow *desperately*, 'you simply must let me do something by way of reparation.'

"I refused sweetly, but as he persisted I let him have my address.

"Of course, we kept our own counsel as to the earlier episodes of the evening. Lord Pabham never advertised the loss of his hyena; when a strictly fruit-eating animal strayed from his park a year or two previously he was called upon to give compensation in eleven cases of sheep-worrying and practically to re-stock his neighbours' poultry-yards, and an escaped hyena would have mounted up to something on the scale of a Government grant. The gipsies were equally *unobtrusive* over their missing offspring; I don't suppose in large *encampments* they really know to a child or two how many they've got."

The Baroness paused *reflectively*, and then continued:

"There was a *sequel* to the adventure, though. I got through the post a charming little diamond broach, with the name Esme set in a sprig of rosemary. Incidentally, too, I lost the friendship of Constance Broddle. You see, when I sold the brooch I quite properly refused to give her any share of the proceeds. I pointed out

Snorted - *Breathe violently*
Desperately - *In urgent need*
Unobtrusive - *Inconspicuous*
Encampments - *Setting up camps*
Sequel - *A literary work, movie, etc.*

that the Esme part of the affair was my own invention, and the hyena part of it belonged to Lord Pabham, if it really was his hyena, of which, of course, I've no proof."

Food For Thought

Why do you think the Baroness lost her friendship with Constance Broddle? Do you think that almost all stories of Saki have a deeper meaning or a hidden element in them? If Yes, you find out the message that has been reflected from this story? Give your answer in five to six lines.

Adrian

A Chapter in Acclimatization

HIs *baptismal* register spoke of him pessimistically as John Henry, but he had left that behind with the other maladies of infancy, and his friends knew him under the front-name of Adrian. His mother lived in Bethnal Green, which was not altogether his fault; one can discourage too much history in one's family, but one cannot always prevent geography. And, after all, the Bethnal Green habit has this virtue - that it is *seldom transmitted* to the next generation. Adrian lived in a roomlet which came under the auspicious constellation of W.

How he lived was to a great extent a mystery even to himself; his struggle for existence probably coincided in many material details with the rather dramatic accounts he gave of it to sympathetic acquaintances. All that is definitely known is that he now and then emerged from the struggle to dine at the Ritz or Carlton, correctly garbed and with a correctly critical appetite. On these occasions he was usually the guest of Lucas Croyden, an amiable worldling, who had three thousand a year and a taste for introducing impossible people to *irreproachable* cookery. Like most men who combine three thousand a year with an uncertain digestion, Lucas was a Socialist, and he argued that you cannot hope to elevate the masses until you have brought plovers' eggs into their lives and taught them to appreciate the difference between coupe Jacques and MacEdoine de fruits. His friends pointed out that it was a doubtful kindness to initiate a boy from behind a *drapery* counter into the *blessedness* of the higher catering, to which Lucas invariably replied that all kindnesses were doubtful. Which was perhaps true.

It was after one of his Adrian evenings that Lucas met his aunt, Mrs. Mebberley, at a fashionable teashop, where the lamp of family life is still kept burning and you meet relatives who might otherwise have slipped your memory.

"Who was that good-looking boy who was dining with you last night?" she asked. "He looked much too nice to be thrown away upon you."

Baptismal - *A trying*
Seldom - *Rauely*
Transmitted - *To spread*
Drapery - *Coverings*

Susan Mebberley was a charming woman, but she was also an aunt.

"Who are his people?" she continued, when the *protege's* name (revised version) had been given her.

"His mother lives at Beth--"

Lucas checked himself on the threshold of what was perhaps a social *indiscretion*.

"Beth? Where is it? It sounds like Asia Minor. Is she mixed up with Consular people?"

"Oh, no. Her work lies among the poor."

This was a side-slip into truth. The mother of Adrian was employed in a laundry.

"I see," said Mrs. Mebberley, "mission work of some sort. And meanwhile the boy has no one to look after him. It's obviously my duty to see that he doesn't come to harm. Bring him to call on me."

"My dear Aunt Susan," *expostulated* Lucas, "I really know very little about him. He may not be at all nice, you know, on further acquaintance."

"He has delightful hair and a weak mouth. I shall take him with me to Homburg or Cairo."

"It's the maddest thing I ever heard of," said Lucas angrily.

"Well, there is a strong strain of madness in our family. If you haven't noticed it yourself all your friends must have."

"One is so dreadfully under everybody's eyes at Homburg. At least you might give him a preliminary trial at Etretat."

"And be surrounded by Americans trying to talk French? No, thank you. I love Americans, but not when they try to talk French. What a blessing it is that they never try to talk English. Tomorrow at five you can bring your young friend to call on me."

And Lucas, realizing that Susan Mebberley was a woman as well as an aunt, saw that she would have to be allowed to have her own way.

Adrian was duly carried abroad under the Mebberley wing; but as a *reluctant concession* to sanity Homburg and other inconveniently fashionable resorts were given a wide berth, and the Mebberley establishment planted itself down in the best hotel at Dohledorf, an Alpine *townlet* somewhere at the back of the Engadine. It was the usual kind of resort, with the usual type of visitors, that one finds over the greater part of Switzerland during the summer

Protege - *A person under the patronage, protection*

Indiscretion - *Imprudence*

Expostulated - *A argue*

Reluctant - *Unwilling*

Townlet - *A small town*

season, but to Adrian it was all unusual. The mountain air, the certainty of regular and abundant meals, and in particular the social atmosphere, affected him much as the *indiscriminating fervour* of a forcing-house might affect a weed that had strayed within its limits. He had been brought up in a world where **breakages** were regarded as crimes and expiated as such; it was something new and altogether *exhilarating* to find that you were considered rather amusing if you smashed things in the right manner and at the recognised hours. Susan Mebberley had expressed the intention of showing Adrian a bit of the world; the particular bit of the world represented by Dohledorf began to be shown a good deal of Adrian.

Lucas got occasional glimpses of the Alpine sojourn, not from his aunt or Adrian, but from the industrious pen of Clovis, who was also moving as a satellite in the Mebberley constellation.

"The entertainment which Susan got up last night ended in disaster. I thought it would. The Grobmayer child, a particularly *loathsome* five-year-old, had appeared as 'Bubbles' during the early part of the evening, and been put to bed during the interval. Adrian watched his opportunity and kidnapped it when the nurse was downstairs, and introduced it during the second half of the entertainment, thinly disguised as a performing pig. It certainly looked very like a pig, and grunted and **slobbered** just like the real article; no one knew exactly what it was, but every one said it was awfully clever, especially the Grobmayers. At the third curtain Adrian pinched it too hard, and it yelled 'Marmar'! I am supposed to be good at descriptions, but don't ask me to describe the sayings and doings of the Grobmayers at that moment; it was like one of the angrier Psalms set to Strauss's music. We have moved to an hotel higher up the valley."

Clovis's next letter arrived five days later, and was written from the Hotel Steinbock.

"We left the Hotel Victoria this morning. It was fairly comfortable and quiet - at least there was an air of repose about it when we arrived. Before we had been in residence twenty-four hours most of the repose had vanished 'like a dutiful bream,' as Adrian expressed it. However, nothing *unduly outrageous* happened till last night, when Adrian had a fit of *insomnia* and amused himself by *unscrewing* and transposing all the bedroom numbers on his floor. He transferred the bathroom label to the adjoining bedroom door, which happened to be that of Frau Hofrath Schilling,

Indiscriminating - *Differentiating*
Fervour - *Zest zeal*
Breakages - *To enliven*
Exhilarating - *Disguesting*
Loathsome - *To let saliva run from the mouth*
Slobbered -

and this morning from seven o'clock onwards the old lady had a stream of involuntary visitors; she was too horrified and scandalised it seems to get up and lock her door. The would-be bathers flew back in confusion to their rooms, and, of course, the change of numbers led them astray again, and the corridor gradually filled with panic-stricken, scantily robed humans, dashing wildly about like rabbits in a **ferret-infested warren.** It took nearly an hour before the guests were all sorted into their respective rooms, and the Frau Hofrath's condition was still causing some anxiety when we left. Susan is beginning to look a little worried. She can't very well turn the boy adrift, as he hasn't got any money, and she can't send him to his people as she doesn't know where they are. Adrian says his mother moves about a good deal and he's lost her address. Probably, if the truth were known, he's had a row at home. So many boys nowadays seem to think that quarrelling with one's family is a recognised occupation."

Lucas's next communication from the travellers took the form of a telegram from Mrs. Mebberley herself. It was sent "reply prepaid," and consisted of a single sentence: "In Heaven's name, where is Beth?"

Indiscriminating -
Differentiating
Fervour - *Zest zeal*
Breakages - *To*
enliven
Exhilarating -
Disguesting
Loathsome - *To let*
saliva run from the
mouth
Slobbered -

Food For Thought

Adrian said to Mrs. Mebberley that he had lost his mother's address as she moved about a great deal. Adrian had no money and nowhere to go. Why do you think Lucas's aunt, Mrs. Mebberley didn't want to keep Adrian with her any longer? Also, why do you think Adrian had fits of insomnia and was very mischievous and troublesome?

A Matter Of Sentiment
~ Saki

IT was the eve of the great race, and scarcely a member of Lady Susan's house-party had as yet a single bet on. It was one of those unsatisfactory years when one horse held a commanding market position, not by reason of any general belief in its crushing *superiority*, but because it was extremely difficult to pitch on any other candidate to whom to pin ones faith. Peradventure II was the favourite, not in the sense of being a popular fancy, but by virtue of a lack of confidence in any one of his rather undistinguished rivals. The brains of club-land were much exercised in seeking out possible merit where none was very obvious to the naked intelligence, and the house-party at Lady Susan's was possessed by the same uncertainty and *irresolution* that infected wider circles.

"It is just the time for bringing off a good coup," said Bertie van Tahn.

"Undoubtedly. But with what?" demanded Clovis for the twentieth time.

The women of the party were just as keenly interested in the matter, and just as helplessly perplexed; even the mother of Clovis, who usually got good racing information from her dressmaker, confessed herself fancy free on this occasion. Colonel Drake, who was professor of military history at a minor *cramming* establishment, was the only person who had a definite selection for the event, but as his choice varied every three hours he was worse than useless as an inspired guide. The crowning difficulty of the problem was that it could only be fitfully and *furtively* discussed. Lady Susan disapproved of racing. She disapproved of many things; some people went as far as to say that she disapproved of most things. Disapproval was to her what *neuralgia* and fancy needlework are to many other women. She disapproved of early morning tea and auction bridge, of skiing and the two-step, of the Russian ballet and the Chelsea Arts Club ball, of the French policy in Morocco and the British policy everywhere. It was not that she was particularly strict or narrow in her views of life, but she had been the eldest sister of a large family of self-indulgent children, and her particular form of *indulgence* had consisted in openly disapproving of the foibles of the

Superiority - *Greater in quality*
Irresolution -*Hesitation*
Cramming - *To memorise information*
Furtively - *Sly and secretive*
Neuralgia - *Sharp, severe never pain*

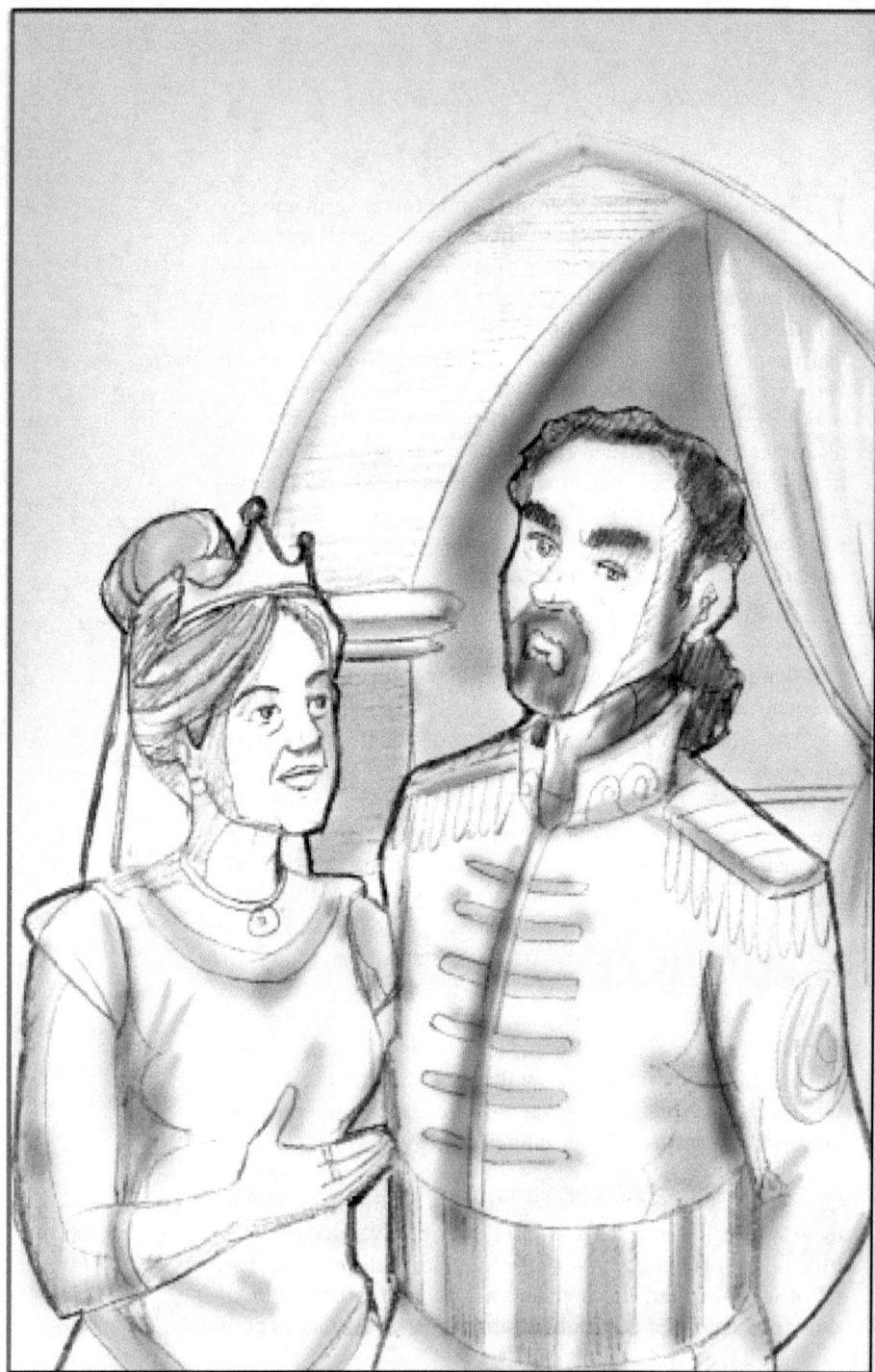

others. Unfortunately the hobby had grown up with her. As she was rich, *influential*, and very, very kind, most people were content to count their early tea as well lost on her behalf. Still, the necessity for hurriedly dropping the discussion of an *enthralling* topic, and suppressing all mention of it during her presence on the scene, was an *affliction* at a moment like the present, when time was slipping away and indecision was the prevailing note.

After a lunch-time of rather strangled and uneasy conversation, Clovis managed to get most of the party together at the further end of the kitchen gardens, on the pretext of admiring the Himalayan *pheasants*. He had made an important discovery. Motkin, the butler, who (as Clovis expressed it) had grown prematurely grey in Lady Susan's service, added to his other excellent qualities an intelligent interest in matters connected with the Turf. On the subject of the forthcoming race he was not illuminating, except in so far that he shared the prevailing unwillingness to see a winner in Peradventure II. But where he *outshone* all the members of the house-party was in the fact that he had a second cousin who was head stable-lad at a neighbouring racing establishment, and usually gifted with much inside information as to private form and possibilities. Only the fact of her ladyship having taken it into her head to invite a house-party for the last week of May had prevented Mr. Motkin from paying a visit of consultation to his relative with respect to the big race; there was still time to cycle over if he could get leave of absence for the afternoon on some *specious* excuse.

"Let's jolly well hope he does," said Bertie van Tahn; "under the circumstances a second cousin is almost as useful as second sight."

"That stable ought to know something, if knowledge is to be found anywhere," said Mrs. Packletide hopefully.

"I expect you'll find he'll echo my fancy for Motorboat," said Colonel Drake.

At this moment the subject had to be hastily dropped. Lady Susan bore down upon them, leaning on the arm of Clovis's mother, to whom she was *confiding* the fact that she disapproved of the craze for Pekingese *spaniels*. It was the third thing she had found time to disapprove of since lunch, without counting her silent and permanent disapproval of the way Clovis's mother did her hair.

"We have been admiring the Himalayan pheasants," said Mrs. Packletide *suavely*.

Influential - *Well-known*

Enthralling - *Captivating*

Affliction - *A condition of great distreass*

Pheasants - *A variety of long-tailed*

Outshone - *To shine more brightly*

Spaniels - *Submissive persons*

"They went off to a bird-show at Nottingham early this morning," said Lady Susan, with the air of one who disapproves of hasty and ill-considered lying.

"Their house, I mean; such perfect *roosting* arrangements, and all so clean," resumed Mrs. Packletide, with an increased glow of enthusiasm. The odious Bertie van Tahn was murmuring audible prayers for Mrs. Packletide's ultimate *estrangement* from the paths of falsehood.

"I hope you don't mind dinner being a quarter of an hour late tonight," said Lady Susan; "Motkin has had an urgent *summons* to go and see a sick relative this afternoon. He wanted to bicycle there, but I am sending him in the motor."

"How very kind of you! Of course we don't mind dinner being put off." The assurances came with *unanimous* and hearty sincerity.

At the dinner-table that night an undercurrent of furtive curiosity directed itself towards Motkin's *impassive countenance.* One or two of the guests almost expected to find a slip of paper concealed in their napkins, bearing the name of the second cousin's selection. They had not long to wait. As the butler went round with the murmured question, "Sherry?" he added in an even lower tone the cryptic words, "Better not." Mrs. Packletide gave a start of alarm, and refused the sherry; there seemed some sinister suggestion in the butler's warning, as though her hostess had suddenly become addicted to the Borgia habit. A moment later the explanation flashed on her that "Better Not" was the name of one of the runners in the big race. Clovis was already pencilling it on his cuff, and Colonel Drake, in his turn, was signalling to every one in hoarse whispers and dumb-show the fact that he had all along fancied "B.N."

Early next morning a *sheaf* of telegrams went Townward, representing the market commands of the house-party and servants' hall.

It was a wet afternoon, and most of Lady Susan's guests hung about the hall, waiting apparently for the appearance of tea, though it was scarcely yet due. The advent of a telegram quickened every one into a flutter of expectancy; the page who brought the telegram to Clovis waited with unusual alertness to know if there might be an answer.

Clovis read the message and gave an exclamation of annoyance.

Hoosting - *Percking*
Estrangement - *To turn away in feedings*
Summons - *A request command*
Unanimous - *Of one mind*
Sheaf - *Any bundle, cluster collection persons*

"No bad news, I hope," said Lady Susan. Every one else knew that the news was not good.

"It's only the result of the Derby," he blurted out; "Sadowa won; an utter outsider."

"Sadowa!" exclaimed Lady Susan; "you don't say so! How remarkable! It's the first time I've ever backed a horse; in fact I disapprove of horse-racing, but just for once in a way I put money on this horse, and it's gone and won."

"May I ask," said Mrs. Packletide, amid the general silence, "why you put your money on this particular horse? None of the sporting prophets mentioned it as having an outside chance."

"Well," said Lady Susan, "you may laugh at me, but it was the name that attracted me. You see, I was always mixed up with the Franco-German war; I was married on the day that the war was declared, and my eldest child was born the day that peace was signed, so anything connected with the war has always interested me. And when I saw there was a horse running in the Derby called after one of the battles in the Franco-German war, I said I *must* put some money on it, for once in a way, though I disapprove of racing. And it's actually won."

There was a general groan. No one groaned more deeply than the professor of military history.

Blurted - *To utter suddenly*
Disapprove - *To deplore, criticize*
Remarkable - *Worthy of notice*

🏂 🏂

Food For Thought

"Sadowa!" exclaimed Lady Susan, "You don't say so! How remarkable! It's the first time I've ever backed a horse." Why do you think Lady Susan betted on this horse when she disliked horse - racing? Does this justify the name of the story or you prefer to suggest something different? If 'Yes', name it and give reasons for your answer.

A Bread And Butter Miss

~ Saki

"**S**tarling Chatter and Oakhill have both dropped back in the betting," said Bertie van Tahn, throwing the morning paper across the breakfast table.

"That leaves Nursery Tea practically favourite," said Odo Finsberry.

"Nursery Tea and Pipeclay are at the top of the betting at present," said Bertie, "but that French horse, Le Five O'Clock, seems to be *fancied* as much as anything. Then there is Whitebait, and the Polish horse with a name like some one trying to *stifle* a sneeze in church; they both seem to have a lot of support."

"It's the most open Derby there's been for years," said Odo.

"It's simply no good trying to pick the winner on form," said Bertie; "one must just trust to luck and inspiration."

"The question is whether to trust to one's own inspiration, or somebody else's. Sporting Swank gives Count Palatine to win, and Le Five O'Clock for a place."

"Count Palatine -- that adds another to our list of perplexities. Good morning, Sir Lulworth; have you a fancy for the Derby by any chance?"

"I don't usually take much interest in turf matters," said Sir Lulworth, who had just made his appearance, "but I always like to have a bet on the Guineas and the Derby. This year, I confess, it's rather difficult to pick out anything that seems markedly better than anything else. What do you think of Snow Bunting?"

"Snow Bunting?" said Odo, with a groan, "there's another of them. Surely, Snow Bunting has no earthly chance?"

"My housekeeper's nephew, who is a shoeing-smith in the mounted section of the Church Lads' Brigade, and an authority on horseflesh, expects him to be among the first three."

"The nephews of housekeepers are invariably optimists," said Bertie; "it's a kind of natural reaction against the professional *pessimism* of their aunts."

"We don't seem to get much further in our search for the *probable* winner," said Mrs. de Claux; "the more I listen to you experts the more hopelessly *befogged* I get."

Fancied - *Imagined*
Stifle - *To quell*
Pessimism - *The tendency to expect the worst*
Probable - *Likely to occur*
Befogged - *Confounded*

"It's all very well to blame us," said Bertie to his hostess; "you haven't produced anything in the way of an inspiration."

"My inspiration consisted in asking you down for Derby week," *retorted* Mrs. de Claux; "I thought you and Odo between you might throw some light on the question of the moment."

Further *recriminations* were cut short by the arrival of Lola Pevensey, who floated into the room with an air of gracious apology.

"So sorry to be so late," she observed, making a rapid tour of *inspection* of the breakfast dishes. "Did you have a good night?" asked her hostess with perfunctory solicitude.

"Quite, thank you," said Lola; "I dreamt a most remarkable dream."

A flutter, indicative of general **boredom**; went round the table. Other people's dreams are about as universally interesting as accounts of other people's gardens, or chickens, or children. "I dreamt about the winner of the Derby," said Lola.

A swift reaction of attentive interest set in.

"Do tell us what you dreamt," came in a chorus.

"The really remarkable thing about it is that I've dreamt it two nights running," said Lola, finally deciding between the **allurements** of sausages and **kedgeree**; "that is why I thought it worth mentioning. You know, when I dream things two or three nights in succession, it always means something; I have special powers in that way. For instance, I once dreamed three times that a winged lion was flying through the sky and one of his wings dropped off, and he came to the ground with a crash; just afterwards the Campanile at Venice fell down. The winged lion is the symbol of Venice, you know," she added for the enlightenment of those who might not be versed in Italian heraldry. "Then," she continued, "just before the murder of the King and Queen of Servia I had a vivid dream of two crowned figures walking into a slaughter-house by the banks of a big river, which I took to be the Danube; and only the other day --"

"Do tell us what you've dreamt about the Derby," interrupted Odo impatiently.

"Well, I saw the finish of the race as clearly as anything; and one horse won easily, almost in a **canter**, and everybody cried out 'Bread and Butter wins! Good old Bread and Butter.' I heard the name distinctly, and I've had the same dream two nights running."

Retorted - *To reply to*
Recriminations - *To return accusations*
Boredom - *Dullness, wearness*
Allurements - *Charms*
Kedgeree - *A cooked dish of rice, fish, hard - boiled eggs*
Canter - *An easy gallop*

"Bread and Butter," said Mrs. de Claux, "now, whatever horse can that point to? Why -- of course; Nursery Tea!"

She looked round with the triumphant smile of a successful *unraveller* of mystery.

"How about Le Five O'Clock?" *interposed* Sir Lulworth.

"It would fit either of them equally well," said Odo; "can you remember any details about the jockey's colours? That might help us."

"I seem to remember a glimpse of lemon sleeves or cap, but I can't be sure," said Lola, after due reflection.

"There isn't a lemon jacket or cap in the race," said Bertie, referring to a list of starters and jockeys; "can't you remember anything about the appearance of the horse? If it were a thick-set animal, this bread and butter would typify Nursery Tea; and if it were thin, of course, it would mean Le Five O'Clock."

"That seems sound enough," said Mrs. de Claux; "do think, Lola dear, whether the horse in your dream was thin or stoutly built."

"I can't remember that it was one or the other," said Lola; "one wouldn't notice such a detail in the excitement of a finish."

"But this was a symbolic animal," said Sir Lulworth; "if it were to *typify* thick or thin bread and butter surely it ought to have been either as bulky and *tubby* as a shire cart-horse; or as thin as a heraldic leopard."

"I'm afraid you are rather a careless dreamer," said Bertie *resentfully*.

"Of course, at the moment of dreaming I thought I was witnessing a real race, not the portent of one," said Lola; "otherwise I should have particularly noticed all helpful details."

"The Derby isn't run till to-morrow," said Mrs. de Claux; "do you think you are likely to have the same dream again to-night? If so; you can fix your attention on the important detail of the animal's appearance."

"I'm afraid I shan't sleep at all to-night," said Lola pathetically; "every fifth night I suffer from *insomnia*, and it's due to-night."

"It's most *provoking*," said Bertie; "of course, we can back both horses, but it would be much more satisfactory to have all our money on the winner. Can't you take a sleeping-draught, or something?"

Unraveller - *To free from complication*
Interposed - *To place between*
Typify - *Short and fat*

"Oakleaves, soaked in warm water and put under the bed, are recommended by some," said Mrs. de Claux.

"A glass of **Benedictine**, with a drop of eau-de-Cologne --" said Sir Lulworth.

"I have tried every known remedy," said Lola, with dignity; "I've been a *martyr* to insomnia for years."

"But now we are being martyrs to it," said Odo sulkily; "I particularly want to land a big coup over this race."

"I don't have insomnia for my own amusement," snapped Lola.

"Let us hope for the best," said Mrs. de Claux soothingly; "to-night may prove an exception to the fifth-night rule."

But when breakfast time came round again Lola reported a blank night as far as visions were concerned.

"I don't suppose I had as much as ten minutes' sleep, and, certainly, no dreams."

"I'm so sorry, for your sake in the first place, and ours as well," said her hostess; "do you think you could induce a short *nap* after breakfast? It would be so good for you -- and you *might* dream something. There would still be time for us to get our bets on."

"I'll try if you like," said Lola; "it sounds rather like a small child being sent to bed in *disgrace*." "I'll come and read the Encyclopaedia Britannica to you if you think it will make you sleep any sooner," said Bertie obligingly.

Rain was falling too steadily to permit of outdoor amusement, and the party suffered considerably during the next two hours from the absolute quiet that was enforced all over the house in order to give Lola every chance of achieving slumber. Even the click of billiard balls was considered a possible factor of disturbance, and the canaries were carried down to the gardener's lodge, while the cuckoo clock in the hall was muffled under several layers of rugs. A notice, "Please do not Knock or Ring," was posted on the front door at Bertie's suggestion, and guests and servants spoke in tragic whispers as though the dread presence of death or sickness had invaded the house. The precautions proved of no *avail*: Lola added a sleepless morning to a *wakeful* night, and the bets of the party had to be *impartially* divided between Nursery Tea and the French *Colt*.

"So provoking to have to split out bets," said Mrs. de Claux, as her guests gathered in the hall later in the day, waiting for the result of the race.

Provoking -
Enraging, vexing
Benedictine - *A monk*
Martyr - *A person who suffers death*
Nap - *Doze, to sleep for a short time*
Disgrace - *The less of respect*

"I did my best for you," said Lola, feeling that she was not getting her due share of gratitude; "I told you what I had seen in my dreams, a brown horse, called Bread and Butter, winning easily from all the rest."

"What?" screamed Bertie, jumping up from his sea, "a brown horse! Miserable woman, you never said a word about it's being a brown horse."

"Didn't I?" faltered Lola; "I thought I told you it was a brown horse. It was certainly brown in both dreams. But I don't see what the colour has got to do with it. Nursery Tea and Le Five O'Clock are both *chestnuts*."

"Merciful Heaven! Doesn't brown bread and butter with a sprinkling of lemon in the colours suggest anything to you?" raged Bertie.

A slow, *cumulative* groan broke from the assembly as the meaning of his words gradually dawned on his hearers.

For the second time that day Lola retired to the seclusion of her room; she could not face the universal looks of reproach directed at her when Whitebait was announced winner at the comfortable price of fourteen to one.

Wakeful - *Watchful, alert*
Colt - *A young male animal of the horse family*
Chestnuts - *Edible nuts tree*
Cumulative - *Growing in quanfity*
Dawned - *To begin to open*
Seclusion - *Solitude*

Food For Thought

Who won the Derby horse-race finally? What was the reaction of Lola and others? Do you believe in betting? Do you feel it's a good pastime or hobby? Support you answer with appropriate reasons.

Tobermory

– Saki

IT was a chill, rain-washed afternoon of a late August day, that indefinite season when partridges are still in security or cold storage, and there is nothing to hunt - unless one is bounded on the north by the Bristol Channel, in which case one may lawfully gallop after fat red stags. Lady Blemley's house-party was not bounded on the north by the Bristol Channel, hence there was a full gathering of her guests round the tea-table on this particular afternoon. And, in spite of the blank-ness of the season and the triteness of the occasion, there was no trace in the company of that fatigued restlessness which means a dread of the pianola and a subdued hankering for auction bridge. The undisguised open-mouthed attention of the entire party was fixed on the homely negative personality of Mr. Cornelius Appin. Of all her guests, he was the one who had come to Lady Blemley with the vaguest reputation. Some-one had said he was "clever," and he had got his invitation in the moderate expectation, on the part of his hostess, that some portion at least of his cleverness would be contributed to the general entertainment. Until tea-time that day she had been unable to discover in what direction, if any, his cleverness lay. He was neither a wit nor a croquet champion, a hypnotic force nor a begetter of amateur theatricals. Neither did his exterior suggest the sort of man in whom women are willing to pardon a generous measure of mental deficiency. He had subsided into mere Mr. Appin, and the Cornelius seemed a piece of transparent baptismal bluff. And now he was claiming to have launched on the world a discovery beside which the invention of gunpowder, of the printing press, and of steam locomotion were inconsiderable trifles. Science had made bewildering strides in many directions during recent decades, but this thing seemed to belong to the domain of miracle rather than to scientific achievement. "And do you really ask us to believe," Sir Wilfrid was saying, "that you have discovered a means for instructing animals in the art of human speech, and that dear old Tobermory has proved your first successful pupil?"

"It is a problem at which I have worked for the last seven-teen years," said Mr. Appin, "but only during the last eight

Indefinite – *Unlimited*
Trite – *Commonplace*
Fatigue – *Exhaustion*
Wit – *Humour*
Amateur – *Inexpert*

or nine months have I been rewarded with glimmerings of success. Of course I have experimented with thousands of animals, but latterly only with cats, those wonderful creatures which have assimilated themselves so marvellously with our civilization while retaining all their highly developed feral instincts. Here and there among cats one comes across an outstanding superior intellect, just as one does among the ruck of human beings, and when I made the acquaintance of Tobermory a week ago I saw at once that I was in contact with a `Beyond-cat' of extraordinary intelligence. I had gone far along the road to success in recent experiments; with Tobermory, as you call him, I have reached the goal."

Mr. Appin concluded his remarkable statement in a voice which he strove to divest of a triumphant inflection. No one said "Rats," though Clovis's lips moved in a monosyllabic contortion which probably invoked those rodents of disbelief.

"And do you mean to say," asked Miss Resker, after a slight pause, "that you have taught Tobermory to say and understand easy sentences of one syllable?"

"My dear Miss Resker," said the wonder-worker patiently, "one teaches little children and savages and backward adults in that piecemeal fashion; when one has once solved the problem of making a beginning with an animal of highly developed intelligence one has no need for those halting methods. Tobermory can speak our language with perfect correctness."

This time Clovis very distinctly said, "Beyond-rats!" Sir Wilfrid was more polite, but equally sceptical. "Hadn't we better have the cat in and judge for ourselves?" suggested Lady Blemley.

Sir Wilfrid went in search of the animal, and the company settled themselves down to the languid expectation of witnessing some more or less adroit drawing room ventriloquism.

In a minute Sir Wilfrid was back in the room, his face white beneath its tan and his eyes dilated with excitement. "By Gad, it's true!"

His agitation was unmistakably genuine, and his hearers started forward in a thrill of awakened interest.

Collapsing into an armchair he continued breathlessly: "I found him dozing in the smoking room and called out to him to come for his tea. He blinked at me in his usual way, and I

Assimilate – *Integrate*
Divest – *Strip*
Triumph – *Victory*
Halt – *Stop*
Languid – *Unhurried*

said, 'Come on, Toby; don't keep us waiting'; and, by Gad! he drawled out in a most horribly natural voice that he'd come when he dashed well pleased! I nearly jumped out of my skin!"

Appin had preached to absolutely incredulous hearers; Sir Wilfred's statement carried instant conviction. A Babel-like chorus of startled exclamation arose, amid which the scientist sat mutely enjoying the first fruit of his stupendous discovery.

In the midst of the clamour Tobermory entered the room and made his way with velvet tread and studied unconcern across to the group seated round the tea-table.

A sudden hush of awkwardness and constraint fell on the company. Somehow there seemed an element of embarrassment in addressing on equal terms a domestic cat of acknowledged mental ability.

"Will you have some milk, Tobermory?" asked Lady Blemley in a rather strained voice.

"I don't mind if I do," was the response, couched in a tone of even indifference. A shiver of suppressed excitement went through the listeners, and Lady Blemley might be excused for pouring out the saucerful of milk rather unsteadily.

"I'm afraid I've spilt a good deal of it," she said apologetically.

"After all, it's not my Axminster," was Tobermory's rejoinder.

Another silence fell on the group, and then Miss Resker, in her best district-visitor manner, asked if the human language had been difficult to learn. Tobermory looked squarely at her for a moment and then fixed his gaze serenely on the middle distance. It was obvious that boring questions lay outside his scheme of life.

"What do you think of human intelligence?" asked Mavis Pellington lamely.

"Of whose intelligence in particular?" asked Tobermory coldly.

"Oh, well, mine for instance," said Mavis, with a feeble laugh.

"You put me in an embarrassing position," said Tobermory, whose tone and attitude certainly did not suggest a shred of embarrassment. "When your inclusion in this house-party was suggested, Sir Wilfrid protested that you were the most

Stupendous –
Astounding
Constraint – *Restraint*

brainless woman of his acquaintance, and that there was a wide distinction between hospitality and the care of the feeble minded. Lady Blemley replied that your lack of brain power was the precise quality which had earned you your invitation, as you were the only person she could think of who might be idiotic enough to buy their old car. You know, the one they call 'The Envy of Sisyphus,' because it goes quite nicely uphill if you push it."

Lady Blemley's protestations would have had greater effect if she had not casually suggested to Mavis only that morning that the car in question would be just the thing for her down at her Devonshire home.

Major Barfield plunged in heavily to effect a diversion.

"How about your carryings-on with the tortoise-shell puss up at the stables, eh?"

The moment he had said it everyone realized the blunder.

"One does not usually discuss these matters in public," said Tobermory frigidly. "From a slight observation of your ways since you've been in this house I should imagine you'd find it inconvenient if I were to shift the conversation on to your own little affairs."

The panic which ensued was not confined to the Major.

"Would you like to go and see if cook has got your dinner ready?" suggested Lady Blemley hurriedly, affecting to ignore the fact that it wanted at least two hours to Tobermory's dinner time. "Thanks," said Tobermory, "not quite so soon after my tea. I don't want to die of indigestion."

"Cats have nine lives, you know," said Sir Wilfrid heartily.

"Possibly", answered Tobermory; "but only one liver."

"Adelaide!" said Mrs. Cornett, "do you mean to encourage that cat to go out and gossip about us in the servants' hall?"

The panic had indeed become general. A narrow ornamental balustrade ran in front of most of the bedroom windows at the Towers, and it was recalled with dismay that this had formed a favourite promenade for Tobermory at all hours, whence he could watch the pigeons - and heaven knew what else besides. If he intended to become reminiscent in his present outspoken strain the effect would be something more than disconcerting. Mrs. Cornett, who spent much time at her toilet table, and whose complexion was reputed to be

Distinct – *Separate*
Precise – *Exact*
Ensue – *Follow*
Narrow – *Thin*
Dismay – *Disappointment*

of a nomadic though punctual disposition, looked as ill at ease as the Major. Miss Scrawen, who wrote fiercely sensuous poetry and led a blameless life, merely displayed irritation; if you are methodical and virtuous in private you don't necessarily want everyone to know it. Bertie van Tahn, who was so depraved at seventeen that he had long ago given up trying to be any worse, turned a dull shade of gardenia white, but he did not commit the error of dashing out of the room like Odo Finsberry, a young gentleman who was understood to be reading for the Church and who was possibly disturbed at the thought of scandals he might hear concerning other people. Clovis had the presence of mind to maintain a composed exterior; privately he was calculating how long it would take to procure a box of fancy mice through the agency of the Exchange and Mart as a species of hush money.

Even in a delicate situation like the present, Agnes Resker could not endure to remain too long in the background.

"Why did I ever come down here?" she asked dramatically.

Tobermory immediately accepted the opening.

"Judging by what you said to Mrs. Cornett on the croquet lawn yesterday, you were out for food. You described the Blemleys as the dullest people to stay with that you knew, but said they were clever enough to employ a first-rate cook; otherwise they'd find it difficult to get anyone to come down a second time."

"There's not a word of truth in it! I appeal to Mrs. Cornett--" exclaimed the discomfited Agnes. "Mrs. Cornett repeated your remark afterwards to Bertie van Tahn," continued Tobermory, "and said, 'That woman is a regular Hunger Marcher; she'd go anywhere for four square meals a day,' and Bertie van Tahn said--"

At this point the chronicle mercifully ceased. Tobermory had caught a glimpse of the big yellow Tom from the Rectory working his way through the shrubbery towards the stable wing. In a flash he had vanished through the open French window.

With the disappearance of his too brilliant pupil Cornelius Appin found himself beset by a hurricane of bitter upbraiding, anxious inquiry, and frightened entreaty. The responsibility for the situation lay with him, and he must prevent matters from becoming worse. Could Tobermory impart his dangerous gift

Deprave – *Corrupt*
Procure – *Acquire*
Endure – *Bear*
Cease – *Stop*
Vanish – *Disappear*

to other cats? was the first question he had to answer. It was possible, he replied, that he might have initiated his intimate friend the stable puss into his new accomplishment, but it was unlikely that his teaching could have taken a wider range as yet.

"Then," said Mrs. Cornett, "Tobermory may be a valuable cat and a great pet; but I'm sure you'll agree, Adelaide, that both he and the stable cat must be done away with without delay."

"You don't suppose I've enjoyed the last quarter of an hour, do you?" said Lady Blemley bitterly. "My husband and I are very fond of Tobermory - at least, we were before this horrible accomplishment was infused into him; but now, of course, the only thing is to have him destroyed as soon as possible."

"We can put some strychnine in the scraps he always gets at dinner time," said Sir Wilfrid, "and I will go and drown the stable cat myself. The coachman will be very sore at losing his pet, but I'll say a very catching form of mange has broken out in both cats and we're afraid of its spreading to the kennels."

"But my great discovery!" expostulated Mr. Appin; "after all my years of research and experiment--" "You can go and experiment on the short-horns at the farm, who are under proper control," said Mrs. Cornett, "or the elephants at the Zoological Gardens. They're said to be highly intelligent, and they have this recommendation, that they don't come creeping about our bedrooms and under chairs, and so forth."

An archangel ecstatically proclaiming the Millennium, and then finding that it clashed unpardonably with Henley and would have to be indefinitely postponed, could hardly have felt more crestfallen than Cornelius Appin at the reception of his wonderful achievement. Public opinion, however, was against him - in fact, had the general voice been consulted on the subject it is probable that a strong minority vote would have been in favour of including him in the strychnine diet.

Defective train arrangements and a nervous desire to see matters brought to a finish prevented an immediate dispersal of the party, but dinner that evening was not a social success. Sir Wilfrid had had rather a trying time with the stable cat and subsequently with the coachman. Agnes Resker ostentatiously limited her repast to a morsel of dry toast, which she bit as though it were a personal enemy; while Mavis Pellington maintained a vindictive silence throughout the meal. Lady Blemley kept up a flow of what she hoped was conversation, but her attention

Impart – *Inform*
Infuse – *Fill*
Sore – *Painful*
Expostulate – *Remonstrate*

was fixed on the doorway. A plateful of carefully dosed fish scraps was in readiness on the sideboard, but sweets and savoury and dessert went their way, and no Tobermory appeared either in the dining room or kitchen.

The sepulchral dinner was cheerful compared with the subsequent vigil in the smoking room. Eating and drinking had at least supplied a distraction and cloak to the prevailing embarrassment. Bridge was out of the question in the general tension of nerves and tempers, and after Odo Finsberry had given a lugubrious rendering of "Melisande in the Wood" to a frigid audience, music was tacitly avoided. At eleven the servants went to bed, announcing that the small window in the pantry had been left open as usual for Tobermory's private use. The guests read steadily through the current batch of magazines, and fell back gradually on the "Badminton Library" and bound volumes of Punch. Lady Blemley made periodic visits to the pantry, returning each time with an expression of listless depression which forestalled questioning.

At two o'clock Clovis broke the dominating silence.

"He won't turn up tonight. He's probably in the local newspaper office at the present moment, dictating the first instalment of his reminiscences. Lady What's-her-name's book won't be in it. It will be the event of the day."

Having made this contribution to the general cheerfulness, Clovis went to bed. At long intervals the various members of the house party followed his example.

The servants taking round the early tea made a uniform announcement in reply to a uniform question. Tobermory had not returned.

Breakfast was, if anything, a more unpleasant function than dinner had been, but before its conclusion the situation was relieved. Tobermory's corpse was brought in from the shrubbery, where a gardener had just discovered it. From the bites on his throat and the yellow fur which coated his claws it was evident that he had fallen in unequal combat with the big Tom from the Rectory.

By midday most of the guests had quitted the Towers, and after lunch Lady Blemley had sufficiently recovered her spirits to write an extremely nasty letter to the Rectory about the loss of her valuable pet.

Vindictive – *Spiteful*
Lugubrious – *Sad*
Frigid – *Chilly*
Combat – *Battle*

Tobermory had been Appin's one successful pupil, and he was destined to have no successor. A few weeks later an elephant in the Dresden Zoological Garden, which had shown no previous signs of irritability, broke loose and killed an Englishman who had apparently been teasing it. The victim's name was variously reported in the papers as Oppin and Eppelin, but his front name was faithfully rendered Cornelius.

"If he was trying German irregular verbs on the poor beast," said Clovis, "he deserved all he got."

Nasty – *Horrid*
Pupil – *Apprentice*

Food For Thought

Cornelius Appin is killed by a zoo's elephant while teaching him to speak. Do you think that he was sensible to have attempted to do so? Give reasons for your answer.

Ministers of Grace "

– Saki

ALthough he was scarcely yet out of his teens, the Duke of Scaw was already marked out as a personality widely differing from others of his caste and period. Not in externals; therein he conformed correctly to type. His hair was faintly reminiscent of Houbigant, and at the other end of him his shoes exhaled the right soupcon of harness room; his socks compelled one's attention without losing one's respect; and his attitude in repose had just that suggestion of Whistler's mother, so becoming in the really young. It was within that the trouble lay, if trouble it could be accounted, which marked him apart from his fellows. The Duke was religious. Not in any of the ordinary senses of the word; he took small heed of High Church or Evangelical standpoints, he stood outside of all the movements and missions and cults and crusades of the day, uncaring and uninterested. Yet in a mystical-practical way of his own, which had served him unscathed and unshaken through the fickle years of boyhood, he was intensely and intensively religious. His family were naturally, though unobtrusively, distressed about it. "I am so afraid it may affect his bridge," said his mother.

The Duke sat in a pennyworth of chair in St. James's Park, listening to the pessimisms of Belturbet, who reviewed the existing political situation from the gloomiest of standpoints.

"Where I think you political spade-workers are so silly," said the Duke, "is in the misdirection of your efforts. You spend thousands of pounds of money, and Heaven knows how much dynamic force of brain power and personal energy, in trying to elect or displace this or that man, whereas you could gain your ends so much more simply by making use of the men as you find them. If they don't suit your purpose as they are, transform them into something more satisfactory."

"Do you refer to hypnotic suggestion?" asked Belturbet, with the air of one who is being trifled with.

"Nothing of the sort. Do you understand what I mean by the verb to koepenick? That is to say, to replace an authority by a spurious imitation that would carry just as much weight for the moment as the displaced original; the advantage, of

Scarce – *Threatened*
Repose – *Peacefulness*
Unscathed –
Unharmed
Fickle – *Indecisive*
Spurious – *FALSE*

course, being that the koepenick replica would do what you wanted, whereas the original does what seems best in its own eyes."

"I suppose every public man has a double, if not two or three," said Belturbet; "but it would be a pretty hard task to koepenick a whole bunch of them and keep the originals out of the way."

"There have been instances in European history of highly successful koepenickery," said the Duke dreamily.

"Oh, of course, there have been False Dimitris and Perkin Warbecks, who imposed on the world for a time," assented Belturbet, "but they personated people who were dead or safely out of the way. That was a comparatively simple matter. It would be far easier to pass oneself off as dead Hannibal than as living Haldane, for instance."

"I was thinking," said the Duke, "of the most famous case of all, the angel who koepenicked King Robert of Sicily with such brilliant results. Just imagine what an advantage it would be to have angels deputizing, to use a horrible but convenient word, for Quinston and Lord Hugo Sizzle, for example. How much smoother the Parliamentary machine would work than at present!" "Now you're talking nonsense," said Belturbet; "angels don't exist nowadays, at least, not in that way, so what is the use of dragging them into a serious discussion? It's merely silly."

"If you talk to me like that I shall just do it," said the Duke.

"Do what?" asked Belturbet. There were times when his young friend's uncanny remarks rather frightened him.

"I shall summon angelic forces to take over some of the more troublesome personalities of our public life, and I shall send the ousted originals into temporary retirement in suitable animal organisms. It's not everyone who would have the knowledge or the power necessary to bring such a thing off--"

"Oh, stop that inane rubbish," said Belturbet angrily; "it's getting wearisome. Here's Quinston coming," he added, as there approached along the almost deserted path the well-known figure of a young Cabinet Minister, whose personality evoked a curious mixture of public interest and unpopularity.

"Hurry along, my dear man," said the young Duke to the Minister, who had given him a condescending nod; "your

Impose – *Levy*
Uncanny – *Weird*
Ousted – *Exiled*
Inane – *Silly*

time is running short," he continued in a provocative strain; "the whole inept crowd of you will shortly be swept away into the world's wastepaper basket."

"You poor little strawberry-leafed nonentity," said the Minister, checking himself for a moment in his stride and rolling out his words spasmodically; "who is going to sweep us away, I should like to know? The voting masses are on our side, and all the ability and administrative talent is on our side too. No power of earth or Heaven is going to move us from our place till we choose to quit it. No power of earth or--"

Belturbet saw, with bulging eyes, a sudden void where a moment earlier had been a Cabinet Minister; a void emphasized rather than relieved by the presence of a puffed-out bewildered-looking sparrow, which hopped about for a moment in a dazed fashion and then fell to a violent cheeping and scolding.

"If we could understand sparrow language," said the Duke serenely, "I fancy we should hear something infinitely worse than 'strawberry-leafed nonentity.' "

"But good Heavens, Eugene," said Belturbet hoarsely, "what has become of-- Why, there he is! How on earth did he get there?" And he pointed with a shaking finger towards a semblance of the vanished Minister, which approached once more along the unfrequented path.

The Duke laughed.

"It is Quinston to all outward appearance," he said composedly, "but I fancy you will find, on closer investigation, that it is an angel under-study of the real article."

The Angel-Quinston greeted them with a friendly smile.

"How beastly happy you two look sitting there!" he said wistfully.

"I don't suppose you'd care to change places with poor little us," replied the Duke chaffingly.

"How about poor little me?" said the Angel modestly. "I've got to run about behind the wheels of popularity, like a spotted dog behind a carriage, getting all the dust and trying to look as if I was an important part of the machine. I must seem a perfect fool to you onlookers sometimes."

"I think you are a perfect angel." said the Duke.

The Angel-that-had-been-Quinston smiled and passed on his way, pursued across the breadth of the Horse Guards Parade

Inept – Incompetent
Void – Invalid
Pursue – Follow

by a tiresome little sparrow that cheeped incessantly and furiously at him.

"That's only the beginning," said the Duke complacently; "I've made it operative with all of them, irrespective of parties."

Belturbet made no coherent reply; he was engaged in feeling his pulse. The Duke fixed his attention with some interest on a black swan that was swimming with haughty, stiff-necked aloofness amid the crowd of lesser water-fowl that dotted the ornamental water. For all its pride of bearing, something was evidently ruffling and enraging it; in its way it seemed as angry and amazed as the sparrow had been.

At the same moment a human figure came along the pathway. Belturbet looked up apprehensively. "Kedzon," he whispered briefly.

"An Angel-Kedzon, if I am not mistaken," said the Duke. "Look, he is talking affably to a human being. That settles it."

A shabbily dressed lounger had accosted the man who had been Viceroy in the splendid East, and who still reflected in his mien some of the cold dignity of the Himalayan snow peaks.

"Could you tell me, sir, if them white birds is storks or halbatrosses? I had an argyment--"

The cold dignity thawed at once into genial friendliness.

"Those are pelicans, my dear sir. Are you interested in birds? If you would join me in a bun and a glass of milk at the stall yonder, I could tell you some interesting things about Indian birds. Right oh! Now the hill-mynah, for instance--"

The two men disappeared in the direction of the bun stall, chatting volubly as they went, and shadowed from the other side of the railed enclosure by a black swan, whose temper seemed to have reached the limit of inarticulate rage.

Belturbet gazed in an open-mouthed wonder after the retreating couple, then transferred his attention to the infuriated swan, and finally turned with a look of scared comprehension at his young friend lolling unconcernedly in his chair. There was no longer any room to doubt what was happening. The "silly talk" had been translated into terrifying action.

"I think a prairie oyster on the top of a stiffish brandy-and-soda might save my reason," said Belturbet weakly, as he limped towards his club.

Complacent – Content
Coherent – Clear
Aloof – Reserved
Rage – Anger

It was late in the day before he could steady his nerves sufficiently to glance at the evening papers. The Parliamentary report proved significant reading, and confirmed the fears that he had been trying to shake off. Mr. Ap Dave, the Chancellor, whose lively controversial style endeared him to his supporters and embittered him, politically speaking, to his opponents, had risen in his place to make an unprovoked apology for having alluded in a recent speech to certain protesting taxpayers as "skulkers." He had realized on reflection that they were in all probability perfectly honest in their inability to understand certain legal technicalities of the new finance laws. The House had scarcely recovered from this sensation when Lord Hugo Sizzle caused a further flutter of astonishment by going out of his way to indulge in an outspoken appreciation of the fairness, loyalty, and straightforwardness not only of the Chancellor, but of all the members of the Cabinet. A wit had gravely suggested moving the adjournment of the House in view of the unexpected circumstances that had arisen.

Belturbet anxiously skimmed over a further item of news printed immediately below the Parliamentary report: "Wild cat found in an exhausted condition in Palace Yard."

"Now I wonder which of them--" he mused, and then an appalling idea came to him. "Supposing he's put them both into the same beast!" He hurriedly ordered another prairie oyster.

Belturbet was known in his club as a strictly moderate drinker; his consumption of alcoholic stimulants that day gave rise to considerable comment.

The events of the next few days were piquantly bewildering to the world at large; to Belturbet, who knew dimly what was happening, the situation was fraught with recurring alarms. The old saying that in politics it's the unexpected that always happens received a justification that it had hitherto somewhat lacked, and the epidemic of startling personal changes of front was not wholly confined to the realm of actual politics. The eminent chocolate magnate, Sadbury, whose antipathy to the Turf and everything connected with it was a matter of general knowledge, had evidently been replaced by an Angel-Sadbury, who proceeded to electrify the public by blossoming forth as an owner of race horses, giving as a reason his matured conviction that the sport was, after all, one which gave healthy open-air

Endear – *Commend*
Embitter – *Disillusion*
Allude – *Mention*
Fraught – *Tense*

recreation to large numbers of people drawn from all classes of the community, and incidentally stimulated the important industry of horse breeding. His colours, chocolate and cream hoops spangled with pink stars, promised to become as popular as any on the Turf. At the same time, in order to give effect to his condemnation of the evils resulting from the spread of the gambling habit among wage-earning classes, who lived for the most part from hand to mouth, he suppressed all betting news and tipsters' forecasts in the popular evening paper that was under his control. His action received instant recognition and support from the Angel-proprietor of the *Evening Views*, the principal rival evening half penny paper, who forthwith issued an ukase decreeing a similar ban on betting news, and in a short while the regular evening Press was purged of all mention of starting prices and probable winners. A considerable drop in the circulation of all these papers was the immediate result, accompanied, of course, by a falling off in advertisement value, while a crop of special betting broadsheets sprang up to supply the newly created want. Under their influence the betting habit became if anything rather more widely diffused than before. The Duke had possibly overlooked the futility of koepenicking the leaders of the nation with excellently intentioned angel under-studies, while leaving the mass of the people in its original condition.

Further sensation and dislocation was caused in the Press world by the sudden and dramatic repprochement which took place between the Angel-Editor of the *Scrutator* and the Angel-Editor of the *Anglian Review*, who not only ceased to criticize and disparage the tone and tendencies of each other's publication, but agreed to exchange editorships for alternating periods. Here again public support was not on the side of the angels; constant readers of the *Scrutator* complained bitterly of the strong meat which was thrust upon them at fitful intervals in place of the almost vegetarian diet to which they had become confidently accustomed; even those who were not mentally averse to strong meat as a separate course were pardonably annoyed at being supplied with it in the pages of the *Scrutator*. To be suddenly confronted with a pungent herring salad when one had attuned oneself to tea and toast, or to discover a richly truffled segment of *pate de foie* dissembled in a bowl of bread and milk, would be an experience that might upset the equanimity of

Rival – *Competing*
Cease – *Stop*
Averse – *Opposed*
Pungent – *Strong*

the most placidly disposed mortal. An equally vehement out-cry arose from the regular subscribers of the *Anglian Review*, who protested against being served from time to time with literary fare which no young person of sixteen could possibly want to devour in secret. To take infinite precautions, they complained, against the juvenile perusal of such eminently innocuous literature was like reading the Riot Act on an un-inhabited island. Both reviews suffered a serious falling-off in circulation and influence. Peace hath its devastations as well as war.

The wives of noted public men formed another element of discomfiture which the young Duke had almost entirely left out of his calculations. It is sufficiently embarrassing to keep abreast of the possible wobblings and veerings-round of a human husband, who, from the strength or weakness of his personal character, may leap over or slip through the barriers which divide the parties; for this reason a merciful politician usually marries late in life, when he has definitely made up his mind on which side he wishes his wife to be socially valuable. But these trials were nothing compared to the bewilderment caused by the Angel-husbands who seemed in some cases to have revolutionized their outlook on life in the interval between breakfast and dinner, with-out premonition or preparation of any kind, and apparently without realizing the least need for subsequent explanation. The temporary peace which brooded over the Parliamentary situation was by no means reproduced in the home circles of the leading statesmen and politicians. It had been frequently and extensively remarked of Mrs. Exe that she would try the patience of an angel; now the tables were reversed, and she unwittingly had an opportunity for discovering that the capacity for exasperating behaviour was not all on one side.

And then, with the introduction of the Navy Estimates, Parliamentary peace suddenly dissolved. It was the old quar-rel between Ministers and the Opposition as to the adequacy or the reverse of the Government's naval programme. The Angel-Quinston and the Angel-Hugo-Sizzle contrived to keep the de-bates free from personalities and pinpricks, but an enormous sensation was created when the elegant lackadaisical Halfan Halfour threatened to bring up fifty thousand stalwarts to wreck the House if the Estimates were not forthwith revised on a Two-Power basis. It was a memorable scene when he rose

Vehement –
Passionate
Devour – *Consume*
Discomfiture –
Embarrassment
Contrive – *Plan*

in his place, in response to the scandalized shouts of his opponents, and thundered forth, "Gentlemen, I glory in the name of Apache."

Belturbet, who had made several fruitless attempts to ring up his young friend since the fateful morning in St. James's Park, ran him to earth one afternoon at his club, smooth and spruce and unruffled as ever.

"Tell me, what on earth have you turned Cocksley Coxon into?" Belturbet asked anxiously, mentioning the name of one of the pillars of unorthodoxy in the Anglican Church. "I don't fancy he believes in angels, and if he finds an angel preaching orthodox sermons from his pulpit while he's been turned into a fox-terrier, he'll develop rabies in less than no time."

"I rather think it was a fox-terrier," said the Duke lazily.

Belturbet groaned heavily, and sank into a chair.

"Look here, Eugene," he whispered hoarsely, having first looked well round to see that no one was within hearing range, "you've got to stop it. Consols are jumping up and down like bronchos, and that speech of Halfour's in the House last night has simply startled everybody out of their wits. And then on the top if it, Thistlebery--"

"What has he been saying?" asked the Duke quickly.

"Nothing. That's just what's so disturbing. Everyone thought it was simply inevitable that he should come out with a great epoch-making speech at this juncture, and I've just seen on the tape that he has refused to address any meetings at present, giving as a reason his opinion that something more than mere speech-making was wanted."

The young Duke said nothing, but his eyes shone with quiet exultation.

"It's so unlike Thistlebery," continued Belturbet; "at least," he said suspiciously, "it's unlike the real Thistlebery--"

"The real Thistlebery is flying about somewhere as a vocally industrious lapwing," said the Duke calmly; "I expect great things of the Angel-Thistlebery," he added.

At this moment there was a magnetic stampede of members towards the lobby, where the tape machines were ticking out some news of more than ordinary import.

"*Coup d'etat* in the North. Thistlebery seizes Edinburgh Castle. Threatens civil war unless Government expands naval programme."

Spruce – *Neat*
Inevitable –
Unavoidable
Exultation –
Happiness
Stampede – *Rush*

In the babel which ensued Belturbet lost sight of his young friend. For the best part of the afternoon he searched one likely haunt after another, spurred on by the sensational posters which the evening papers were displaying broadcast over the West End. General Baden-Baden mobilizes Boy-Scouts. Another *coup d'etat* feared. Is Windsor Castle safe?" This was one of the earlier posters, and was followed by one of even more sinister purport: "Will the Test match have to be postponed?" It was this disquietening question which brought home the real seriousness of the situation to the London public, and made people wonder whether one might not pay too high a price for the advantages of party government. Belturbet, questing round in the hope of finding the originator of the trouble, with a vague idea of being able to induce him to restore matters to their normal human footing, came across an elderly club acquaintance who dabbled extensively in some of the more sensitive market securities. He was pale with indignation, and his pallor deepened as a breathless newsboy dashed past with a poster inscribed: "Premier's constituency harried by moss-troopers. Halfour sends encouraging telegram to rioters. Letchworth Garden City threatens reprisals. Foreigners taking refuge in Embassies and National Liberal Club."

"This is devils' work!" he said angrily.

Belturbet knew otherwise.

At the bottom of St. James's Street a newspaper motor-cart, which had just come rapidly along Pall Mall, was surrounded by a knot of eagerly talking people, and for the first time that afternoon Belturbet heard expressions of relief and congratulation.

It displayed a placard with the welcome announcement: "Crisis ended. Government gives way. Important expansion of naval programme."

There seemed to be no immediate necessity for pursuing the quest of the errant Duke, and Belturbet turned to make his way homeward through St. James's Park. His mind, attuned to the alarms and excursions of the afternoon, became dimly aware that some excitement of a detached nature was going on around him. In spite of the political ferment which reigned in the streets, quite a large crowd had gathered to watch the unfolding of a tragedy that had taken place on the shore of the ornamental water. A large black swan, which had recently shown signs of a savage and dangerous disposition, had suddenly attacked a young gentleman who was walking by the water's

Ensue – *Follow*
Sinister – *Ominous*
Pallor – *Paleness*
Quest – *Mission*
Attune – *Adjust*

edge, dragged him down under the surface, and drowned him before anyone could come to his assistance. At the moment when Belturbet arrived on the spot several park-keepers were engaged in lifting the corpse into a punt. Belturbet stooped to pick up a hat that lay near the scene of the struggle. It was a smart soft felt hat, faintly reminiscent of Houbigant.

More than a month elapsed before Belturbet had sufficiently recovered from his attack of nervous prostration to take an interest once more in what was going on in the world of politics. The Parliamentary Session was still in full swing, and a General Election was looming in the near future. He called for a batch of morning papers and skimmed rapidly through the speeches of the Chancellor, Quinston, and other Ministerial leaders, as well as those of the principal Opposition champions, and then sank back in his chair with a sigh of relief. Evidently the spell had ceased to act after the tragedy which had overtaken its invoker. There was no trace of angel anywhere.

Tragedy – *Disaster*
Punt – *Boot*
Reminiscent – *Significant*

🏂 🏂

Food For Thought

Why did Belturbet heave a sigh of relief after going through the speeches of the Chancellor, Quinston and other ministerial leaders? 'Evidently, the spell had ceased to act after the tragedy which had overtaken its invoker.' What was the spell and what was the tragedy all about? Explain.

The Music on the Hill

~ Saki

SYlvia Seltoun ate her breakfast in the morning room at Yessney with a *pleasant* sense of ultimate *victory*, such as a *fervent* Ironside might have permitted himself on the *morrow* of Worcester fight. She was scarcely *pugnacious* by temperament, but belonged to that more successful class of fighters who are pugnacious by circumstance. Fate had willed that her life should be occupied with a series of small struggles, usually with the odds slightly against her, and usually she had just managed to come through winning. And now she felt that she had brought her hardest and certainly her most important struggle to a successful issue. To have married Mortimer Seltoun, "Dead Mortimer" as his more intimate enemies called him, in the teeth of the cold *hostility* of his family, and in spite of his unaffected indifference to women, was indeed an achievement that had needed some determination and adroitness to carry through; yesterday she had brought her victory to its concluding stage by wrenching her husband away from town and its group of satellite watering places and "settling him down," in the vocabulary of her kind, in this remote wood-girt manor farm which was his country house.

"You will never get Mortimer to go," his mother had said carpingly, "but if he once goes he'll stay; Yessney throws almost as much a spell over him as Town does. One can understand what holds him to Town, but Yessney--" and the dowager had shrugged her shoulders.

There was a somber almost *savage* wildness about Yessney that was certainly not likely to appeal to town-bred tastes, and Sylvia, notwithstanding her name, was accustomed to nothing much more sylvan than "leafy Kensington." She looked on the country as something excellent and wholesome in its way, which was apt to become troublesome if you encouraged it overmuch. *Distrust* of town life had been a new thing with her, born of her marriage with Mortimer, and she had watched with satisfaction the *gradual* fading of what she called "the Jermyn-Street-look" in his eyes as the woods and heather of Yessney had closed in on them yester night. Her will power and *strategy* had *prevailed*; Mortimer would stay. Outside the

Fervent – Keen
Pugnacious – Aggressive
Temperament – Nature
Sombre – Sooty
Hostility - Enemity
Gradual - Slow but Steady
Savage - Wild
Distrust - Doubt ones Credibility

morning room windows was a triangular slope of turf, which the indulgent might call a lawn, and beyond its low hedge of neglected fuschia bushes a steeper slope of heather and bracken dropped down into cavernous combes overgrown with oak and yew. In its wild open savagery there seemed a stealthy linking of the joy of life with the terror of unseen things. Sylvia smiled complacently as she gazed with a School-of-Art appreciation at the landscape, and then of a sudden she almost **shuddered**.

"It is very wild," she said to Mortimer, who had joined her; "one could almost think that in such a place the worship of Pan had never quite died out."

"The worship of Pan never has died out," said Mortimer. "Other newer gods have drawn aside his votaries from time to time, but he is the Nature-God to whom all must come back at last. He has been called the Father of all the Gods, but most of his children have been stillborn."

Sylvia was religious in an **honest**, vaguely devotional kind of way, and did not like to hear her beliefs spoken of as mere aftergrowths, but it was at least something new and hopeful to hear Dead Mortimer speak with such energy and **conviction** on any subject.

"You don't really believe in Pan?" she asked **incredulously**.

"I've been a fool in most things," said Mortimer quietly, "but I'm not such a fool as not to believe in Pan when I'm down here. And if you're wise you won't disbelieve in him too boastfully while you're in his country."

It was not till a week later, when Sylvia had exhausted the attractions of the woodland walks round Yessney, that she **ventured** on a tour of **inspection** of the farm buildings. A farmyard suggested in her mind a scene of cheerful bustle, with churns and flails and smiling dairymaids, and teams of horses drinking knee-deep in duck-crowded ponds. As she wandered among the gaunt grey buildings of Yessney manor farm her first impression was one of crushing stillness and **desolation**, as though she had happened on some lone **deserted** homestead long given over to owls and cobwebs; then came a sense of **furtive** watchful hostility, the same shadow of unseen things that seemed to lurk in the wooded combes and coppices. From behind heavy doors and shuttered windows came the restless stamp of hoof or rasp of chain halter, and at times a muffled bellow from some stalled beast. From a distant comer a shaggy dog watched her

Shuddered - *Shaken*
Turf - *Grass*
Heather - *Ash*
Complacently - *Contently*
Incredulously - *In amazement*

with intent unfriendly eyes; as she drew near it slipped quietly into its kennel, and slipped out again as noiselessly when she had passed by. A few hens, questing for food under a rick, stole away under a gate at her approach. Sylvia felt that if she had come across any human beings in this wilderness of barn and byre they would have fled wraith-like from her gaze. At last, turning a corner quickly, she came upon a living thing that did not fly from her. Astretch in a pool of mud was an *enormous* sow, gigantic beyond the town-woman's wildest computation of swine flesh, and speedily alert to *resent* and if necessary repel the unwonted *intrusion*. It was Sylvia's turn to make an *unobtrusive* retreat. As she threaded her way past rickyards and cowsheds and long blank walls, she started suddenly at a strange sound - the echo of a boy's laughter, golden and equivocal. Jan, the only boy employed on the farm, a tow-headed, wizen-faced yokel, was visibly at work on a potato clearing half-way up the nearest hill side, and Mortimer, when questioned, knew of no other probable or possible begetter of the hidden *mockery* that had *ambushed* Sylvia's retreat. The memory of that untraceable echo was added to her other impressions of a furtive sinister "something" that hung around Yessney.

Of Mortimer she saw very little; farm and woods and trout streams seemed to *swallow* him up from dawn till dusk. Once, following the direction she had seen him take in the morning, she came to an open space in a nut copse, further shut in by huge yew trees, in the centre of which stood a stone pedestal *surmounted* by a small bronze figure of a youthful Pan. It was a beautiful piece of workmanship, but her attention was chiefly held by the fact that a newly cut bunch of grapes had been placed as an offering at its feet. Grapes were none too plentiful at the manor house, and Sylvia snatched the bunch angrily from the pedestal. Contemptuous annoyance *dominated* her thoughts as she *strolled* slowly homeward, and then gave way to a sharp feeling of something that was very near fright; across a thick tangle of undergrowth a boy's face was scowling at her, brown and beautiful, with unutterably evil eyes. It was a lonely pathway, all pathways round Yessney were lonely for the matter of that, and she sped forward without waiting to give a closer *scrutiny* to this sudden *apparition*. It was not till she had reached the house that she discovered that she had dropped the bunch of grapes in her flight.

Shaggy – *Unkempt*
Questing – *Hunt*
Byre – *Stable*
Equivocal – *Unclear*
Apparition - *A supernatural appearance of a person thing*
Surmounted - *To prevail over*
Strolled - *Walked leisurely*

"I saw a youth in the wood today," she told Mortimer that evening, "brown-faced and rather handsome, but a scoundrel to look at. A gipsy lad, I suppose."

"A reasonable theory," said Mortimer, "only there aren't any gipsies in these parts at present."

"Then who was he?" asked Sylvia, and as Mortimer appeared to have no theory of his own she passed on to recount her finding of the *votive* offering.

"I suppose it was your doing," she observed; "it's a harmless piece of lunacy, but people would think you **dreadfully** silly if they knew of it."

"Did you *meddle* with it in any way?" asked Mortimer.

"I - I threw the grapes away. It seemed so silly," said Sylvia, watching Mortimer's *impassive* face for a sign of annoyance.

"I don't think you were **wise** to do that," he said reflectively. "I've heard it said that the Wood Gods are rather horrible to those who molest them."

"Horrible perhaps to those that believe in them, but you see I don't," *retorted* Sylvia.

"All the same," said Mortimer in his even, *dispassionate* tone, "I should avoid the woods and orchards if I were you, and give a wide berth to the horned beasts on the farm."

It was all nonsense, of course, but in that lonely wood-girt spot nonsense seemed able to *rear* a bastard brood of uneasiness.

"Mortimer," said Sylvia suddenly, "I think we will go back to town some time soon."

Her victory had not been so complete as she had supposed; it had carried her on to ground that she was already *anxious* to quit.

"I don't think you will ever go back to town," said Mortimer. He seemed to be paraphrasing his mother's prediction as to himself.

Sylvia noted with *dissatisfaction* and some self-*contempt* that the course of her next afternoon's ramble took her instinctively clear of the network of woods. As to the horned cattle, Mortimer's warning was scarcely needed, for she had always regarded them as of doubtful neutrality at the best. Her imagination unsexed the most matronly dairy cows and turned them into bulls liable to "see red" at any moment. The ram who fed in the narrow paddock below the orchards she had *adjudged*,

Gipsy – *Nomad*
Lunacy – *Madness*
Horned – *Punch*
Neutrality –
Impartiality
Votive - *Offered,*
dedicated
Impassive - *Calm,*
screen
Meddle - *Interfere,*
Intervene
Retorted - *Reply*
sharply

after *ample* and cautious probation, to be of *docile* temper; today, however, she decided to leave his docility untested, for the usually *tranquil* beast was roaming with every sign of restlessness from corner to corner of his meadow. A low, fitful piping, as of some reedy flute, was coming from the depth of a neighbouring *copse*, and there seemed to be some *subtle* connection between the animal's restless pacing and the wild music from the wood. Sylvia turned her steps in an upward direction and climbed the heather-clad slopes that stretched in rolling shoulders high above Yessney. She had left the piping notes behind her, but across the wooded combes at her feet the wind brought her another kind of music, the straining bay of hounds in full chase. Yessney was just on the outskirts of the Devon-and-Somerset country, and the hunted deer sometimes came that way. Sylvia could presently see a dark body, breasting hill after hill, and sinking again and again out of sight as he crossed the combes, while behind him steadily swelled that relentless chorus, and she grew tense with the excited sympathy that one feels for any hunted thing in whose *capture* one is not directly interested. And at last he broke through the outermost line of oak scrub and fern and stood panting in the open, a fat September stag carrying a well-furnished head. His obvious course was to drop down to the brown pools of Undercombe, and thence make his way towards the red deer's favoured sanctuary, the sea. To Sylvia's surprise, however, he turned his head to the upland slope and came lumbering resolutely onward over the heather. "It will be dreadful," she thought, "the hounds will pull him down under my very eyes." But the music of the pack seemed to have died away for a moment, and in its place she heard again that wild piping, which rose now on this side, now on that, as though urging the failing stag to a final effort. Sylvia stood well aside from his path, half hidden in a thick growth of whortle bushes, and watched him swing stiffly upward, his flanks dark with sweat, the *coarse* hair on his neck showing light by contrast. The pipe music shrilled suddenly around her, seeming to come from the bushes at her very feet, and at the same moment the great beast slewed round and bore directly down upon her. In an instant her pity for the hunted animal was changed to wild terror at her own danger; the thick heather roots mocked her scrambling efforts at flight, and she looked frantically downward for a *glimpse* of oncoming hounds. The huge antler spikes were within a

Paddock – *Enclosure*
Docility – *Obedience*
Copse – *Grove*
Sympathy – *Kindness*
Ample - *Enough*
Tranquit - *Peaceful*

few yards of her, and in a flash of *numbing* fear she remembered Mortimer's warning, to beware of horned beasts on the farm. And then with a quick *throb* of joy she saw that she was not alone; a human figure stood a few *paces* aside, knee-deep in the *whortle* bushes.

"Drive it off!" she shrieked. But the figure made no answering movement.

The antlers drove straight at her breast, the acrid smell of the hunted animal was in her nostrils, but her eyes were filled with the *horror* of something she saw other than her oncoming death. And in her ears rang the *echo* of a boy's laughter, golden and *equivocal*.

Food For Thought

Do you think Sylvia was right in snatching the bunch of grapes angrily from the stone pedestal of a Wood God or a youthful Pan God? What was the consequence of doing this? One should never meddle with or disrespect one's religious sentiments. Do you agree with this statement? Give reasons as to why/why not?

Whortle - A kind of berry (fruit), whortleberry
Numbing - Deadening
Throb – Thump
Paces – Footstep
Echo – Reverberance

The Hedgehog

- Saki

A "Mixed Double" of young people were contesting a game of lawn tennis at the Rectory garden party; for the past five-and-twenty years at least mixed doubles of young people had done exactly the same thing on exactly the same spot at about the same time of year. The young people changed and made way for others in the course of time, but very little else seemed to *alter*. The present players were sufficiently *conscious* of the social nature of the occasion to be concerned about their clothes and appearance, and sufficiently sport-loving to be keen on the game. Both their efforts and their appearance came under the fourfold scrutiny of a quartet of ladies sitting as official spectators on a bench immediately commanding the court. It was one of the accepted conditions of the Rectory garden party that four ladies, who usually knew very little about tennis and a great deal about the players, should sit at that particular spot and watch the game. It had also come to be almost a tradition that two ladies should be *amiable*, and that the other two should be Mrs. Dole and Mrs. Hatch-Mallard.

"What a singularly *unbecoming* way Eva Jonelet has taken to doing her hair in," said Mrs. Hatch-Mallard; "it's ugly hair at the best of times, but she needn't make it look *ridiculous* as well. Some one *ought* to tell her."

Eva Jonelet's hair might have escaped Mrs. Hatch-Mallard's *condemnation* if she could have forgotten the more glaring fact that Eva was Mrs. Dole's favourite niece. It would, perhaps, have been a more comfortable arrangement if Mrs. Hatch-Mallard and Mrs. Dole could have been asked to the Rectory on separate occasions, but there was only one garden party in the course of the year, and neither lady could have been *omitted* from the list of invitations without hopelessly *wrecking* the social peace of t he parish.

"How pretty the yew trees look at this time of year," interposed a lady with a soft, silvery voice that suggested a chinchilla muff painted by Whistler.

"What do you mean by this time of year?" demanded Mrs. Hatch-Mallard. "Yew trees look beautiful at all times of the year. That is their great charm."

Alter – *Change*
Scrutiny – *Inspection*
Amiable – *Friendly*
Unbecoming – *Incorrect*
Ridiculous - *Funny*
Conscious - *Aware*
Condemnation - *Defame*
Wrecking - *Ruining*

"Yew trees never look anything but hideous under any circumstances or at any time of year," said Mrs. Dole, with the slow, *emphatic* relish of one who contradicts for the pleasure of the thing. "They are only fit for graveyards and cemeteries."

Mrs. Hatch-Mallard gave a *sardonic snort*, which, being translated, meant that there were some people who were better fitted for cemeteries than for garden parties.

"What is the score, please?" asked the lady with the chinchilla voice.

The desired information was given her by a young gentleman in spotless white flannels, whose general toilet effect suggested *solicitude* rather than anxiety.

"What an *odious* young cub Bertie Dykson has become!" pronounced Mrs. Dole, remembering suddenly that Bertie was a favourite with Mrs. Hatch-Mallard. "The young men of today are not what they used to be twenty years ago."

"Of course not," said Mrs. Hatch-Mallard; "twenty years ago Bertie Dykson was just two years old, and you must expect some difference in appearance and manner and conversation between those two periods."

"Do you know," said Mrs. Dole, confidentially, "I shouldn't be surprised if that was intended to be clever."

"Have you any one interesting coming to stay with you, Mrs. Norbury?" asked the chinchilla voice, hastily; "you generally have a house party at this time of year."

"I've got a most interesting woman coming," said Mrs. Norbury, who had been mutely struggling for some chance to turn the conversation into a safe channel; "an old *acquaintance* of mine, Ada Bleek —."

"What an ugly name," said Mrs. Hatch-Mallard.

"She's descended from the de la Bliques, an old Huguenot family of Touraine, you know."

"There weren't any Huguenots in Touraine," said Mrs. Hatch-Mallard, who thought she might safely *dispute* any fact that was three hundred years old.

"Well, anyhow, she's coming to stay with me," continued Mrs. Norbury, bringing her story quickly down to the present day, "she arrives this evening, and she's highly *clairvoyant*, a seventh daughter of a seventh daughter, you now, and all that sort of thing."

Hideous – *Ugly*
Emphatic – *Forceful*
Sardonic – *Mocking*
Clairvoyant - *Clear sighted*
Snort - *Loud, harsh sound*
Solicitude - *Anxiety, Worry concern*

"How very interesting," said the chinchilla voice; "Exwood is just the right place for her to come to, isn't it? There are supposed to be several ghosts there."

"That is why she was so anxious to come," said Mrs. Norbury; "she put off another engagement in order to accept my invitation. She's had visions and dreams, and all those sort of things, that have come true in a most marvellous manner, but she's never actually seen a ghost, and she's longing to have that experience. She belongs to that Research Society, you know."

"I expect she'll see the unhappy Lady Cullumpton, the most famous of all the Exwood ghosts," said Mrs. Dole; "my ancestor, you know, Sir Gervase Cullumpton, murdered his young bride in a fit of jealousy while they were on a visit to Exwood.

He strangled her in the stables with a stirrup leather, just after they had come in from riding, and she is seen sometimes at dusk going about the lawns and the stable yard, in a long green habit, moaning and trying to get the thong from round her throat. I shall be most interested to hear if your friend sees --"

"I don't know why she should be expected to see a trashy, traditional *apparition* like the so-called Cullumpton ghost, that is only vouched for by housemaids and tipsy stable boys, when my uncle, who was the owner of Exwood, committed suicide there under the most tragical circumstances, and most certainly *haunts* the place."

"Mrs. Hatch-Mallard has evidently never read Popple's County History," said Mrs. Dole icily, "or she would know that the Cullumpton ghost has a wealth of evidence behind it --"

"Oh, Popple!" exclaimed Mrs. Hatch-Mallard scornfully; "any rubbishy old story is good enough for him. Popple, indeed! Now my uncle's ghost was seen by a Rural Dean, who was also a Justice of the Peace.

I should think that would be good enough testimony for any one. Mrs. Norbury, I shall take it as a deliberate personal *affront* if your clairvoyant friend sees any other ghost except that of my uncle."

"I daresay she won't see anything at all; she never has yet, you know," said Mrs. Norbury hopefully.

Anxious – Nervous
Marvellous – Wonderful
Longing – Desire
Vouched – Answer for
Affront - To confront
Apparition - A ghostly appearance
Haunts - To visit habitually as a spirit
Lamented - Mourned Grieved

"It was a most unfortunate topic for me to have broached," she *lamented* afterwards to the owner of the chinchilla voice; "Exwood belongs to Mrs. Hatch-Mallard, and we've only got it on a short lease. A nephew of hers has been wanting to live there for some time, and if we offend her in any way she'll refuse to renew the lease. I sometimes think these garden parties are a mistake."

The Norburys played bridge for the next three nights till nearly one o'clock; they did not care for the game, but it reduced the time at their guest's disposal for undesirable ghostly visitations.

"Miss Bleek is not likely to be in a frame of mind to see ghosts," said Hugo Norbury, "if she goes to bed with her brain *awhirl* with royal spades and no trumps and grand slams."

"I've talked to her for hours about Mrs. Hatch-Mallard's uncle," said his wife, "and pointed out the exact spot where he killed himself, and invented all sorts of impressive details, and I've found an old portrait of Lord John Russell and put it in her room, and told her that it's supposed to be a picture of the uncle in middle age. If Ada does see a ghost at all it certainly ought to be old Hatch-Mallard's. At any rate, we've done our best."

The precautions were in *vain*. On the third morning of her stay, Ada Bleek came down late to breakfast, her eyes looking very tired, but *ablaze* with excitement, her hair done anyhow, and a large brown volume hugged under her arm.

"At last I've seen something supernatural!" she exclaimed, and gave Mrs. Norbury a *fervent* kiss, as though in **gratitude** for the opportunity afforded her.

"A ghost!" cried Mrs. Norbury, "not really!"

"Really and unmistakably!"

"Was it an oldish man in the dress of about fifty years ago?" asked Mrs. Norbury hopefully.

"Nothing of the sort," said Ada; "it was a white hedgehog."

"A white hedgehog!" exclaimed both the Norburys, in tones of *disconcerted* astonishment.

"A huge white hedgehog with *baleful* yellow eyes," said Ada; "I was lying half asleep in bed when suddenly I felt a sensation as of something *sinister* and unaccountable passing through the room.

Lease – *Rent*
Ablaze – *On fire*
Supernatural – *Paranormal*
Vain - *Very proud*
Fervent - *Intensely passionate, ardent*
Gratitude - *Graterfulness*

I sat up and looked around, and there, under the window, I saw an evil, creeping thing, a sort of monstrous hedgehog, of a dirty white colour, with black, **loathsome** claws that clicked and scraped along the floor, and narrow, yellow eyes of indescribable evil.

It *slithered* along for a yard or two, always looking at me with its cruel, hideous eyes, then, when it reached the second window, which was open it clambered up the sill and vanished.

I got up at once and went to the window; there wasn't a sign of it anywhere. Of course, I knew it must be something from another world, but it was not till I turned up Popple's chapter on local traditions that I realised what I had seen."

She turned eagerly to the large brown volume and read: "'Nicholas Herison, an old miser, was hung at Batchford in 1763 for the murder of a farm lad who had accidentally discovered his secret *hoard*. His ghost is supposed to *traverse* the countryside, appearing sometimes as a white owl, sometimes as a huge white hedgehog.'"

"I expect you read the Popple story overnight, and that made you *think* you saw a hedgehog when you were only half awake," said Mrs. Norbury, hazarding a *conjecture* that probably came very near the truth.

Ada scouted the possibility of such a solution of her apparition.

"This must be hushed up," said Mrs. Norbury quickly; "the servants-"

"Hushed up!" exclaimed Ada, *indignantly*; "I'm writing a long report on it for the Research Society."

It was then that Hugo Norbury, who is not naturally a man of brilliant resource, had one of the really useful inspirations of his life.

"It was very wicked of us, Miss Bleek," he said, "but it would be a shame to let it go further. That white hedgehog is an old joke of ours; stuffed albino hedgehog, you know, that my father brought home from Jamaica, where they grow to *enormous* size.

We hide it in the room with a string on it, run one end of the string through the window; then we pull if from below and it comes scraping along the floor, just as you've described,

Slithered – *Glide*
Clambered – *Climb*
Traverse – *Cross*
Conjecture – *Guess*
Enormous - *Huge*
Hoard - *To accumulate, Reserre*
Indignantly - *Resentful, angry*

and finally jerks out of the window. Taken in heaps of people; they all read up Popple and think it's old Harry Nicholson's ghost; we always stop them from writing to the papers about it, though. That would be carrying matters too far."

Mrs. Hatch-Mallard renewed the lease in due course, but Ada Bleek has never renewed her friendship.

Food For Thought

What was actually the huge white hedgehog? Why did Miss Ada Bleek think that it was a ghost? How do you think Miss Ada Bleek felt when Mr. Hugo Norbury narrated his old joke? Write a story similar to this one and speak about your own experience when somebody made a fool of you.

Jerks – Sudden breaks, push
Heaps – Pile, Stocks
Lease – A contract lending land, building, etc.

www.ingramcontent.com/pod-product-compliance
Lightning Source LLC
LaVergne TN
LVHW021620080426
835510LV00019B/2671